EVERYMAN,
I WILL GO WITH THEE
AND BE THY GUIDE,
IN THY MOST NEED
TO GO BY THY SIDE

EVERYMAN'S LIBRARY
POCKET POETS

Rimbaud

Poems

Translated by
Paul Schmidt

E V E R Y M A N ' S   L I B R A R Y

P O C K E T   P O E T S

Alfred A. Knopf · New York · Toronto

THIS IS A BORZOI BOOK

PUBLISHED BY ALFRED A. KNOPF, INC.

This selection by Peter Washington first published in
Everyman's Library, 1994
English language translation copyright © 1975 by Paul Schmidt
Published by arrangement with HarperCollins Publishers, Inc.
All rights reserved.
Third printing

ISBN 0-679-43321-X
LC 94-2496

Library of Congress Cataloging-in-Publication Data
Rimbaud, Arthur, 1854–1891.
[Poems.   English]
Poems / Arthur Rimbaud.
p.   cm.—(Everyman's library pocket poets)
Includes bibliographical references.
ISBN 0-679-43321-X
1. Rimbaud, Arthur, 1854–1891—Translations into English.
I. Title. II. Series.
PQ2637.R5A2   1994   94-2496
841'.8—dc20   CIP

Typography by Peter B. Willberg

Typeset in the UK by MS Filmsetting Ltd., Frome, Somerset

Printed in Great Britain at Mackays of Chatham PLC
by arrangement with Associated Agencies Ltd.

ARTHUR RIMBAUD

CONTENTS

OPHELIA

I

Where the stars sleep in the calm black stream,
Like some great lily, pale Ophelia floats,
Slowly floats, wound in her veils like a dream.
– Half heard in the woods, halloos from distant
   throats.

A thousand years has sad Ophelia gone
Glimmering on the water, a phantom fair;
A thousand years her soft distracted song
Has waked the answering evening air.

The wind kisses her breasts and shakes
Her long veils lying softly on the stream;
The shivering willows weep upon her cheeks;
Across her dreaming brows the rushes lean.

The wrinkled water lilies round her sigh;
And once she wakes a nest of sleeping things
And hears the tiny sound of frightened wings;
Mysterious music falls from the starry sky.

II

O pale Ophelia, beautiful as snow!
Yes, die, child, die, and drift away to sea!
For from the peaks of Norway cold winds blow
And whisper low of bitter liberty;

For a breath that moved your long heavy hair
Brought strange sounds to your wandering thoughts;
Your heart heard Nature singing everywhere,
In the sighs of trees and the whispering of night.

For the voice of the seas, endless and immense,
Breaks your young breast, too human and too sweet;
For on an April morning a pale young prince,
Poor lunatic, sat wordless at your feet!

Sky! Love! Liberty! What a dream, poor young
Thing! you sank before him, snow before fire,
Your own great vision strangling your tongue,
Infinity flaring in your blue eye!

III

And the Poet says that by starlight you came
To pick the flowers you loved so much, at night,
And he saw, wound in her veils like a dream,
Like some great lily, pale Ophelia float.

THE HANGED MEN DANCE

> On old one–arm, black scaffolding,
> The hanged men dance;
> The devil's skinny advocates,
> Dead soldiers' bones.

Beelzebub jerks ropes about the necks
Of small black dolls who squirm against the sky;
With slaps, with whacks and cuffs and kicks
He makes them dance an antique roundelay!

Excited jumping jacks, they join thin arms;
Black organ lofts, their fretwork breasts
That once beat fast at beauteous damsels' charms
Now clack together in a perverse embrace.

Hurrah the jolly dancers, whose guts are gone!
About the narrow planks they jerk and prance!
Beelzebub roars the rasping fiddles' song!
Hop! They cannot tell the battle from the dance!

Hard heels, that never wear out shoes!
They've all put off their overcoat of skin;
What's left beneath is hardly worth excuse –
Their skulls are frail and white beneath the rain.

A crow provides a crest for these cracked heads,
A strip of flesh shakes on a skinny chin;
They swing about in somber skirmishes
Like heroes, stiff, their armor growing thin.

And the breeze blows for the skeletons' ball!
The gibbet groans like an organ of iron;
In violet forests the wolves wail;
The distant sky flames with hell's own fires!

Oh, shake me these dark commanders down!
Who slyly rake through broken fingertips
Love's rosary across their pale ribs:
This is no monastery, you dead men!

And there in the midst of the danse macabre
One wild skeleton leaps in the scarlet clouds,
Stung with madness like a rearing horse
With the rope pulled stiff above his head.

He tightens bony fingers on his cracking knees
With squeals that make a mock of dead men's groans,
And, like a puppet flopping in the breeze,
Whirls in the dance to the sound of clacking bones.

> On old one-arm, black scaffolding,
> The hanged men dance;
> The devil's skinny advocates,
> Dead soldiers' bones.

KIDS IN A DAZE

Black against the fog and snow,
Against a grating all aglow,
Their asses spread,

Five kids – poor things! – squat and shake,
To watch a happy Baker bake
Hot golden bread.

They watch his white arms beat
The dough, and feel the heat
Of the bright stoves.

They hear the Baker softly hum
And hear a crackling sound come
From the baking loaves.

They are transfixed; they do not dare
Disturb the fragrant glowing air,
Warm as a mother's breast.

For a rich man's holiday he bakes
Golden rolls and pies and cakes –
A sugary feast!

And then beneath the smoky roof
They hear a song from a savory loaf
– Just like a bird!

The warm window steams and glows,
And they squat in their ragged clothes,
Their senses blurred –

They even think that they're rich, too –
Poor Baby Jesuses in a row
As the snow falls;

They stick their little noses in
Through the grating, moaning something
Through the holes

In a daze, saying prayers
And bending toward the lights
Of paradise,

So hard they split their pants,
And their shirttails dance
In a wind like ice.

TARTUFE CHASTISED

Fanning flames in a lovesick heart beneath
His chaste black robe, content, and hand in glove,
One day he went to church smirking with love,
Gray, dribbling faith from a mouth without teeth;

One day he went to church, 'to pray'; a crook
Grabbed him and whispered some dirty words in
His holy ear, and with a nasty look
Removed his chaste black robe from his damp skin!

Chastisement! With all his buttons undone
And the list of indulgences he'd won
Unraveling on his breast, Tartufe went white!

He prayed and confessed in an awful fright!
But the man ran away with all his clothes –
Ugh! Tartufe stood naked from head to toes!

FIRST EVENING

Her clothes were almost off;
Outside, a curious tree
Beat a branch at the window
To see what it could see.

Perched on my enormous easy chair,
Half nude, she clasped her hands.
Her feet trembled on the floor,
As soft as they could be.

I watched as a ray of pale light,
Trapped in the tree outside,
Danced from her mouth
To her breast, like a fly on a flower.

I kissed her delicate ankles.
She had a soft, brusque laugh
That broke into shining crystals –
A pretty little laugh.

Her feet ducked under her chemise;
'Will you please stop it! ...'
But I laughed at her cries –
I knew she really liked it.

Her eyes trembled beneath my lips;
They closed at my touch.
Her head went back; she cried:
'Oh, *really!* That's too much!

'My dear, I'm warning you ...'
I stopped her protest with a kiss
And she laughed, low –
A laugh that wanted more than this ...

Her clothes were almost off;
Outside, a curious tree
Beat a branch at the window
To see what it could see.

ROMANCE

I

Nobody's serious when they're seventeen.
On a nice night, the hell with beer and lemonade
And the café and the noisy atmosphere!
You walk beneath the linden trees on the promenade.

The lindens smell lovely on a night in June!
The air is so sweet that your eyelids close.
The breeze is full of sounds – they come from the town –
And the scent of beer, and the vine, and the rose...

II

You look up and see a little scrap of sky,
Dark blue and far off in the night,
Stuck with a lopsided star that drifts by
With little shivers, very small and white...

A night in June! Seventeen! Getting drunk is fun.
Sap like champagne knocks your head awry...
Your mind drifts; a kiss rises to your lips
And flutters like a little butterfly...

III

Your heart Crusoes madly through novels, anywhere,
When through the pale pool beneath a street light,
A girl goes by with the *most* charming air,
In the grim shadow of her father's dark coat.

And since she finds you marvelously naïve,
While her little heels keep tapping along
She turns, with a quick bright look ...
And on your lips, despairing, dies your song.

IV

You are in love. Rented out till fall.
You are in love. Poetic fires ignite you.
Your friends laugh; they won't talk to you at all.
Then one night, the goddess deigns to write you!

That night ... you go back to the café, to the noisy
    atmosphere;
You sit and order beer, or lemonade ...
Nobody's serious when they're seventeen,
And there are linden trees on the promenade.

BY THE BANDSTAND
Railroad Square, Charleville

On Railroad Square, laid out in little spots of lawn,
Where all is always order, the flowers and trees,
All the puffing bourgeois, strangling in the heat,
Parade their envious nonsense on Thursday afternoon.

In the middle of the garden a military band is
Playing, helmets jiggling to 'Lady of Spain';
By the benches in front dawdle the dandies;
The Notary dangles from his own watch chain.

Retired bourgeois blink through their glasses at the noise;
Fat stuffed clerks drag along their fat stuffed wives;
By them scurry others, fussy elephant boys,
Flapping like signs with nothing to advertise.

On the green benches, clumps of retired grocers
Poke at the sand with their knob-top canes,
Gravely talk of treaties, of war, move closer,
Take snuff from little boxes, then begin: 'Which means ...'

Flattening his global bottom on a bench,
A bourgeois with a shiny-buttoned gut – Flemish, not
    French –
Sucks his smelly pipe, whose flaky tobacco
Overflows – 'It's real imported stuff, you know ...'

On the green grass, slum kids yell and throw stones;
Chewing on roses, fresh-faced young soldiers
Feel sexy at the sound of slide trombones,
And wink at babies on pretty nurses' shoulders.

– And I go running after girls beneath the trees,
In my messy clothes, just like a student:
They know exactly what I'm after, and their eyes
On me can't hide the things I know they want.

I don't say anything: I just keep staring
At the white skin on their necks, their tousled hair,
At what's beneath the silly dresses they're wearing
That show their backs and leave their shoulders bare.

Pretty soon I see a shoe, then a stocking ...
I put it all together: shoulders, back, hips;
They think I'm strange; they whisper, laughing,
    mocking ...
And my brutal wishes bite their little lips ...

FAUN'S HEAD

Among the leaves, green curtain stained with gold,
Among the tremulous leaves, the flowery
Tangled bower, like a sudden kiss revealed,
Bright rent in this exquisite tapestry,

Glitter the eyes of a frightened faun
Who bites the red flowers with his small white teeth.
Brown and bloody as the dregs of wine,
His lips part in laughter beneath a leaf.

Then, like a squirrel, he turns and disappears,
But his laughter lingers still along the leaves,
And, shaken as a startled chaffinch soars,
The Golden Kiss of the Woods is left in peace.

THE SIDEBOARD

It is a high, carved sideboard made of oak.
The dark old wood, like old folks, seems kind;
Its drawers are open, and its odors soak
The darkness with the scent of strong old wine.

Its drawers are full, a final resting place
For scented, yellowed linens, scraps of clothes
For wives or children, worn and faded bows,
Grandmothers' collars made of figured lace;

There you will find old medals, locks of gray
Or yellow hair, and portraits, and a dried bouquet
Whose perfume mingles with the smell of fruit.

– O sideboard of old, you know a great deal more
And could tell us your tales, yet you stand mute
As we slowly open your old dark door.

THE TEASE

In the dark brown dining room, whose heavy air
Had a comfortable smell of fruit and varnish,
I got a plate full of some local Belgian dish
Or other, and stretched out long in my lazy chair.

Content and still, I ate and listened to the clock.
Just then the kitchen door flew open wide
And the servant-girl came in, I don't know why –
The top of her dress undone, her hair pulled back.

And while she put a finger to her cheek,
All rosy-white and velvet, like a peach,
And made a face just like a five-year-old,

To make things easier she shifted the dishes;
And then she said – and I knew she wanted kisses! –
Real low: 'Feel *that*: my cheek has got so cold ...'

AT THE GREEN CABARET
(five in the afternoon)

A week of walking had torn my boots to shreds.
I finally got to Charleroi and came
To the Green Cabaret; I ordered bread
And butter and a piece of half-cold ham.

I felt good, stretched out my legs under
A table and looked at the silly tapestries
Hanging on the wall. And what a wonder,
When a girl with enormous tits and shining eyes

– Hell, a kiss would never scare *her* off! –
Laughed as she brought me the bread and butter
And a fancy platter of ham, half-cold –

Ham, all pink and white, it had a garlic
Taste – and filled my mug with beer, whose froth
A ray of fading sunlight turned to gold.

WANDERING

I ran away, hands stuck in pockets that seemed
All holes; my jacket was a holey ghost as well.
I followed you, Muse! Beneath your spell,
Oh, la, la, what glorious loves I dreamed!

I tore my shirt; I threw away my tie.
Dreamy Hop o' my Thumb, I made rhymes
As I ran. I slept out most of the time.
The stars above me rustled through the sky.

I heard them on the roadsides where I stopped
Those fine September nights, when the dew dropped
On my face and I licked it to get drunk.

I made up rhymes in dark and scary places,
And like a lyre I plucked the tired laces
Of my worn-out shoes, one foot beneath my heart.

DREAM IN WINTERTIME
To ... her

All winter we'll wander in a red wagon
With cushions of blue.
Nice and warm. With a nest of creepy kisses
Just for us two.

You shut your eyes and won't look out the window
Where shadows lurk:
Hordes of black wolves and black demons and
    nightmares
Inhabit the dark.

And then in panic suddenly you feel
A little kiss, like a scared spider, crawl
Across your cheek ...

You turn to me to help you find the beast,
And of course I promise to do my best,
If it takes all week ...

WHAT NINA ANSWERED

He: Just the two of us together,
        Okay? We could go
Through the fresh and pleasant weather
        In the cool glow

Of the blue morning, washed in
        The wine of day . . .
When all the love-struck forest
        Quivers, bleeds

From each branch; clear drops tremble,
        Bright buds blow,
Everything opens and vibrates;
        All things grow.

You rush about, and alfalfa
        Stains your white gown,
As the shadows beneath your eyelids
        Fade in the clear dawn.

Madly in love with the country,
        You sprinkle about
Like shining champagne bubbles
        Your crazy laugh:

Laughing at me, and I'd be brutal
        And I'd grab your hair
Like this — how beautiful,
        Oh! — In the air

Your strawberry-raspberry taste,
        Your flowery flesh!
Laughing at the wind that kissed
        You like a thief,

At the eglantine you stumble in
        (It loves you, too!)
Laughing most of all, little dummy,
        At me with you!

Just the two of us together,
        Our voices joined,
Slowly we'd wander farther
        Into the wood . . .

Then, like the girl in the fairy tale
        You'd start to faint;
You'd tell me to carry you
        With half a wink . . .

I'd carry you quivering
    Beneath a tree;
A bird nearby is whistling:
    'Who loves to lie with me ...'

I'd whisper into your mouth,
    Put you to bed,
Your body curled like a baby's,
    Drunk on the blood

That flows, blue, beneath the softness
    Of skin like snow;
Whispering about those shameless
    Things ... You know ...

Our woods smell of springtime,
    And the sun
Powders with gold their vision
    Vermilion and green.

At night? We'll return on the shining
    White road that goes
Idly along, like a flock browsing;
    Around us grows

The blue grass of lovely orchards,
    Their bending trees;
For miles around as you wander
    You smell their scent!

We'll get back to the village
    Just at dusk,
And smell the odor of milking
    On the evening air,

And the warm smell of stables
    Full of manure,
Of a calm rhythm of breathing
    And of broad backs

Pale in the light of a lantern;
    And there below
A cow drops dung, dignified
    And slow.

Grandmother's eyeglasses sparkle
    As she peers
In her prayerbook; a tin bucket
    Of beer

Foams in front of long pipes
    That happily expel
Clouds of smoke; the flapping faces,
    Smoking still,

Shove in ham by forkfuls:
    Lots, then more;
The fire lights the cupboards
    And beds on the floor.

The fat shiny bottom
    Of a husky kid
Crawling to lick the dishes,
    His tow head

Tousled by a huge hound dog
    With a soft growl,
Who licks the round features
    Of the dear child . . .

Dark, on the edge of her chair,
    An arrogant profile –
An old woman spinning
    By the fire.

What things we'll see, my darling,
    In those farms,
By those bright fires sparkling
    In dark windowpanes!

Then, tiny, hidden under
    A lilac bush, fresh
And shady: a little window
    Just for us . . .

I love you! Come! Come for
    A beautiful walk!
You will come, won't you? What's more . . .

SHE: *And be late for work?*

THE CUSTOMS MEN

The redneck cops, the big fat ones who leer,
Retired sailors, soldiers, Legionnaires,
Are nothing next to the Great Concessionaires:
The cops who guard our virginal frontier.

With pipes and knives and clubs – but without fear –
They take their German Shepherds out in pairs
To catch the simple smuggler unawares.
They chuckle in the drooling atmosphere.

They bring forest deities their modern laws.
They round up wandering Fausts and Diavolos.
'The game is up! Let's put those bundles down!'

And when these great men have to search the young,
Watch out! They hate to let 'Delinquents' pass –
God help you, when the Customs grabs your ass!

'YOU DEAD OF NINETY-TWO AND NINETY-THREE'

> 'Frenchmen of 1870,
> Bonapartists, Republicans, remember
> your ancestors of 1792, etc. . . .'
> PAUL DE CASSAGNAC, in *The Nation*

You dead of ninety-two and ninety-three,
Pale in freedom's powerful embrace,
Whose wooden shoes once crushed a yoke that weighs
On the soul and brow of all humanity;

Men made great by agony, ecstatic men,
Ragged men, hearts moved by love alone,
Soldiers whom Death, unflinching Lover, has sown
In our wasted furrows, to flourish again;

Men whose blood restored our tarnished greatness,
Dead men of Italy, of Valmy, of Fleurus,
A million Christs with somber gentle eyes;

We have let you fall with our Republic, we
Have bent our backs by Imperial decree –
And now our *newspapers* praise you to the skies!

THE BRILLIANT VICTORY OF SAAREBRUCK

> Won to the Accompaniment of Cries of
> 'Long Live the Emperor!'
> *(A Belgian print, in full color,*
> *on sale in Charleroi for 35 centimes)*

In the middle, the Emperor, an apotheosis
Of blue and gold, rides off, stiff as a rod,
Seeing the world through rosy-colored glasses.
Our Dear Old Daddy, glorious as God!

Below, the draftees, waking from their nap
Beside a gilded tent and a great red gun,
Get up politely. Pitou puts on his cap,
And seeing his Chief, he cries with joy: 'We've won!'

On the right, Dumanet, leaning on the stock
Of his rifle, rubbing his shivering, shaven neck,
Yells: 'The Emperor!' His neighbor's mouth stays shut . . .

A helmet appears – a sunrise out of place;
But Boquillon, in blue, flat on his face,
Heisting his ass, says: 'Emperor of *what?*'

EVIL

While the red-stained mouths of machine guns ring
Across the infinite expanse of day;
While red or green, before their posturing King,
The massed battalions break and melt away;

And while a monstrous frenzy runs a course
That makes of a thousand men a smoking pile –
Poor fools! – dead, in summer, in the grass,
On Nature's breast, who meant these men to smile;

There is a God, who smiles upon us through
The gleam of gold, the incense-laden air,
Who drowses in a cloud of murmured prayer,

And only wakes when weeping mothers bow
Themselves in anguish, wrapped in old black shawls –
And their last small coin into his coffer falls.

ASLEEP IN THE VALLEY

A small green valley where a slow stream runs
And leaves long strands of silver on the bright
Grass; from the mountaintop stream the sun's
Rays; they fill the hollow full of light.

A soldier, very young, lies open-mouthed,
A pillow made of ferns beneath his head,
Asleep; stretched in the heavy undergrowth,
Pale in his warm, green, sun-soaked bed.

His feet among the flowers, he sleeps. His smile
Is like an infant's – gentle, without guile.
Ah, Nature, keep him warm; he may catch cold.

The humming insects don't disturb his rest;
He sleeps in sunlight, one hand on his breast,
At peace. In his side there are two red holes.

ANGRY CAESAR

This man, pale, walks the flowering lawns,
Dressed in black, cigar between his teeth.
The pale man thinks about the Tuileries
In flower ... and at times his dead eye flames.

His twenty years of orgy have made him drink!
He told himself: 'I will extinguish Liberty
As I put out a candle – softly, politely ...'
Liberty lives again! He feels worn out.

They've caught him. Now what name trembles
On his silent lips? What quick regret?
No one will know: the Emperor's eye is dead.

He sees again, perhaps, the man in the pince-nez ...
And watches drifting from his lighted cigar,
Like evenings at St. Cloud, a thin blue haze.

PARISIAN WAR CRY

Spring is at hand, for lo,
Within the city's garden plots
The government's harvest is beginning to grow –
But the gardeners call the shots!

O May! What bare-assed ecstasy!
Sèvres, Meudon, Bagneux, Asnières,
Hear our Farmer-Generals, busy
Planting in the empty air!

Guns and sabers glitter in parade,
Bright-mouthed weapons pointing straight ahead –
It's a treat for them to beat their feet
In the mud of a river running red!

Never, never now will we move back
From our barricades, our piles of stone;
Beneath their clubs our blond skulls crack
In a dawn that was meant for us alone.

Like Eros, politicians hover overhead,
Their shadows withering the flowers:
Their bombs and fires paint our garden red:
Their beetle-faced forces trample ours . . .

They are all great friends of the Grand Truc!
Their chief in his gladiolus bed blinks
Back his tears, puts on a sorrowful look,
Sniffs smoke-filled air, and winks.

The city's paving stones are hot
Despite the gasoline you shower,
And absolutely, now, right now, we've got
To find a way to break your power!

Bourgeois, bug-eyed on their balconies,
Shaking at the sound of breaking glass,
Can hear trees falling on the boulevards
And, far off, a shivering scarlet clash.

THE HANDS OF JEANNE-MARIE

Jeanne-Marie has powerful hands,
Dark hands summertime has tanned,
Hands pale as a dead man's hands.
Are these the hands of Juana?

Were they rubbed with dark creams
Beside voluptuous lagoons?
Were they dangled in clear streams
To dissipate reflected moons?

Have they drunk from savage
Skies, calm upon quiet knees?
Have they rolled cigars?
Dealt in diamonds?

At the feet of the Madonna
Have they crumpled flowers of gold?
With the black blood of belladonna
Their glistening palms are filled.

Hands that hunt auroral
Beetles, bluenesses bumbling
Over nectaries? Hands
That pour out poison?

Ah, what dream seizes
And convulses them?
Some unimagined dream of Asias,
Khenghavars or Sion?

These are no orange-seller's hands,
Hands darkened as a god's disguise;
These hands have never washed the clothes
Of heavy children without eyes.

These are not like the hands at home,
Nor the hardened hands of girls who work
In factories, whose fat faces burn
In sunlight sick with oily smoke.

These are the benders of backbones,
Hands that have never done wrong,
Hands fatal as machinery,
Strong as a horse is strong!

Shaking like bright furnaces,
Their flesh cries out the 'Marseillaise,'
Shakes shivering to silences,
And never quavers Kyries!

They'll break your necks, you whores,
Strangle you, daughters of night;
Crush your hands, you countesses,
Your hands painted red and white.

The brilliance of these hands in love
Dazzles the skulls of baby lambs!
At the joint of each rich knuckle
The bright sun's ruby gleams!

A stain, a splash of populace,
Darkens them like yesterday's breast;
The back of these Hands is the place
All your ardent Rebels have kissed!

Marvelously pale in the sun's
Love-provoking light, they hauled
The bronze barrels of machine guns
Across Paris in revolt!

And sometimes on these sacred Hands,
Hands made fists, where our mouths remain
Trembling, our intoxicated mouths,
Sounds the bright clinking of a chain!

And then how strange, you Angel-hands,
That sudden shudder deep inside,
When they wish to crush your fingers
To drench your Hands in blood!

PARISIAN ORGY

Cowards, behold her now! Pour from your trains!
The fiery breath of the sky sweeps down
Along boulevards barbarians have stained.
Behold the Holy City, in the setting sun!

Go on! Beware of buildings still on fire!
Here are the quais, the boulevards, and here
Are houses, beneath bright streaks of sky
That last night were stuck with stars of fire!

Board up the dying palaces, the empty halls;
The ancient trembling daylight cools your eyes.
Behold this rusty troop of wriggling souls:
Your mad haggard faces and your wild cries!

Hordes of bitches in heat gulp cataplasms;
The scream of houses full of gold commands: Steal!
Gorge! Behold, the joyful night in inky spasms
Descends upon the street. O desolate drinkers,

Drink! And then when mad blinding light stabs
Through the dripping heap of orgy at your sides,
Will you not slaver slowly, silent, still,
Into your glasses, staring at empty distances?

Drink to the Empress and her cascading ass!
Hear the sound of retching, of drunken yells!
Hear burning nights recoil beneath this mass
Of howling idiots, old men, perverted fools!

O filthy hearts, O monstrous stinking mouths,
Perform your functions harder, louder, wilder!
Pour wine, grovel like beasts upon these tables . . .
Your stomachs melt with shame, O Conquerors!

Open your nostrils, smell this maddening stench!
Let poisons soak the channels of your throats!
Over your childish heads, lowering his folded hands,
The Poet speaks: 'O cowards, now cry out!

'See how you forage in the belly of Woman,
And still you fear her, wait for her to moan,
For convulsions that will crush the foul nest
You force in crusted slime upon her breast.

'Syphilitics, madmen, kings and fools,
Do you think Paris cares, the monstrous whore?
Cares for your souls, your bodies, poisons, rags?
She will shake you off, rotten, wretched, foul,

'And when you lie crushed, groaning in your bowels,
Dead flesh crying for gold, hysterical,
The scarlet courtesan with battle-swollen tits
Above your groans will clench her fiery fists!'

When your feet have danced in savage anger,
Paris! When so many knives have stabbed your breast,
When you lie prostrate, still in your clear eyes
Shines the innocence of the regenerate beast,

O sorrowful city! O city now struck dumb,
Head and heart stretched out in paleness
In endless doorways thrown wide by Time;
City the dismal Past can only bless:

Body galvanized for sufferings yet to come,
You drink once more the bitter draught that saves!
Within your veins you feel the white worms swarm;
Within your perfect love a freezing finger moves!

And the feeling isn't bad. The worms, the white worms
Cannot pervert the Progress of your mouth,
Nor the Stryx close up the eyes of Caryatids
Whose tears of astral gold rain from the azure South.

The Poet will gather the sobs of monstrous Criminals,
The Convict's hate, the cries of the Accursed;
The streams of his love will flay all womankind.
His poems will soar: Behold, thieves! Do your worst!

Society, all is restored: orgies, the old
Groans choke the lupanars once more,
Maddened gaslight on blood-stained walls
Lights the blue dark with a sinister glare!

And though we shrink to see you thus laid waste,
Though never thus before was a city
Made abominable in Nature's face,
The Poet speaks: 'Great is the sight of your Beauty!'

The storm has christened you supreme poetry;
An enormous stirring raises you; death groans.
Your task is lifted from you, Holy City!
Stridencies resound in your trumpet of bronze.

CROWS

Lord, when the open field is cold,
When in the battered villages
The endless angelus dies –
Above the dark and drooping world
Let the empty skies disclose
Your dear, delightful crows.

Armada dark with harsh cries,
Your nests are tossed by icy winds!
Along the banks of yellowed ponds,
On roads where crumbling crosses rise,
In cold and gray and mournful weather
Scatter, hover, dive together!

In flocks above the fields of France
Where yesterday's dead men lie,
Wheel across the winter sky;
Recall our black inheritance!
Let duty in your cry be heard,
Mournful, black, uneasy bird.

Yet in that oak, you saints of God,
Swaying in the dying day,
Leave the whistling birds of May
For those who found, within that wood
From which they will not come again,
That every victory is vain.

EVENING PRAYER

I spend my life sitting, like an angel in a barber's chair,
Holding a beer mug with deep-cut designs,
My neck and gut both bent, while in the air
A weightless veil of pipe smoke hangs.

Like steaming dung within an old dovecote
A thousand Dreams within me softly burn:
From time to time my heart is like some oak
Whose blood runs golden where a branch is torn.

And then, when I have swallowed down my Dreams
In thirty, forty mugs of beer, I turn
To satisfy a need I can't ignore,

And like the Lord of Hyssop and of Myrrh
I piss into the skies, a soaring stream
That consecrates a patch of flowering fern.

THE SITTERS

Black with warts, picked with pox, eyelids all green,
Their knobbly fingers curled around their balls,
Skulls smeared with nastinesses, obscene
As the crud that grows on rotten walls;

A kind of epileptic embrace screws
Their skinny skeletons to the black bones
Of their chairs; and there for days and days
Their old feet wriggle on the rickety rungs.

These old men always entangled in their chairs
Watch their skin in the hot sun corrode;
They stare at a window where wet snow glares,
Or shake with the painful shaking of a toad.

And their Chairs take care of them; their asses
Are worn, but the straw seats cup them like a palm,
And the soul of suns gone by still burns
In those strips of straw, those rotting grains.

The Sitters gnaw their knees; green piano players,
Their fingers move in rhythm beneath their chairs;
They hear themselves splashing a sad barcarole,
And their heads go floating off on waves of love.

Oh, don't get up! It's just a little flood . . .
They heave themselves in waves, snarling like wet cats;
— Are they mad! Their shoulderblades unfold
And their pants puff out over their fat butts.

You hear them bumping bald heads against the walls;
They catch you walking down the long dark halls,
And if you look, the buttons on their flies
Watch you like a lot of hungry eyes!

And they have these fast invisible hands
That get you, and their eyes have a poisonous stare;
You feel like a beaten puppy dog, and
You sweat, caught in that awful corridor!

They sit back down, fists drowned in dirty cuffs,
Thinking of those who made them get up.
In agitated lumps, from dawn to dusk,
The goiters quiver in their nervous necks.

A fit of sleep; they pull their eyeshades low;
They fold their arms and dream of fucking chairs;
They dream of having baby chairs that grow
In groups: in quartets, trios, and in pairs.

Flowers of ink spurt commas in showers
That hover above them, over their bent buds,
Like dragonflies that buzz a bed of flowers ...
And the prickle of straw makes their cocks hard.

SQUATTING

Later, when he feels his stomach upset,
Brother Milotus, with a glance at the skylight
Where the sun, bright as a new-polished pot,
Gives him a headache and dazzles his eyesight,
Beneath the bedclothes moves his priestly gut.

He flaps about beneath his grayish sheets
And then gets up and gropes to find his basin,
Scared as an old man who's swallowed his teeth,
Because he has his thick nightshirt to fasten
Around his gut before he can proceed!

He shivers and squats, with his toes tucked up
Beneath him, shaking in sunshine that smears cracker-
Yellow on windowpanes papered at the top;
The old man's nose — it glows like scarlet lacquer —
Sniffs the sunshine, like some fleshy polyp.

The old man stews by the fire, dribbling lip
Over his stomach; his thighs slip, then settle;
He feels his scorched britches, his dying pipe;
Something that was once a bird burbles a little
In a stomach soft as a heap of tripe.

A tangle of banged-up furniture, deep
In greasy rags, bulging like filthy bellies;
Fantastic stools like clumsy toads are heaped
In corners: sideboards have singers' gullets
Gaping with horrid appetite for sleep.

A sickening heat stifles the narrow room;
The old man's brain is stuffed with scraps from junk
    heaps.
He hears hairs growing deep in his damp skin,
And sometimes burps, and rather gravely hiccups,
And jolts the shaky stool he squats upon ...

And at night the brightness of the moon's light,
Dribbling on the curves of his ass, discloses
A dark shadow that falls across a bright
Pink snowdrift, pink as blushing summer roses ...
An odd nose traces Venus through the night.

POOR PEOPLE IN CHURCH

Bent on wooden benches, in church corners
Warmed by the stink of their breath, their eyes dim
In the altar's glitter, turned to the rafters
Where twenty pious faces howl a hymn;

Sniffing the smell of wax like baking bread,
Happy, humble as dogs with a beaten air,
The Poor raise to God, their savior and lord,
An endless, obstinate, ludicrous prayer.

The women like to sit on the smooth seats
After the six black days God puts them through.
They cradle in ill-fitting, twisted coats
Funny kids who cry, their faces turning blue.

Sloppy breasts hang out: these eaters of soup
– Prayer in their eyes, without a prayer within –
Watch a slovenly parade; a gawky group
Of girls in shapeless hats of unknown origin.

Outside – cold, and hunger, and horny husbands.
It's all right here. Another hour, then nameless pain.
Yet all around them, coughs, moans, whispers:
Little clusters of dewlapped women whine.

Those beggars are there, and the epileptics
We avoided yesterday as we crossed the road;
And, nosing their way through ancient prayerbooks,
The blind men dogs drag through our yards.

They dribble faith, and mouth a stupid, begging love,
Reciting their endless complaint to Jesus –
Who dreams in a yellow glow, far above
Skinny failures and potbellied successes,

Far from the meatlike smells, the moldy clothes,
The dark shuffling farce and its repulsive mime;
– Then the litany flowers with elegant woes
And mysteries flutter toward the sublime,

And from out of the nave where sunlight dies,
With stupid silks, sour smiles, and liver complaints,
Come ladies from the Better Side of Town – Jesus! –
Trailing yellowed fingers in the holy water fonts.

VENUS ANADYOMENE

Out of what seems a coffin made of tin
A head protrudes; a woman's, dark with grease –
Out of a bathtub! – slowly; then a fat face
With ill-concealed defects upon the skin.

Then, streaked and gray, a neck; a shoulderblade,
A back – irregular, with indentations –
Then round loins emerge, and slowly rise;
The fat beneath the skin seems made of lead;

The spine is somewhat reddish; then, a smell,
Strangely horrible; we notice above all
Some microscopic blemishes in front . . .

Horribly beautiful! A title: CLARA VENUS;
Then the huge bulk heaves, and with a grunt
She bends and shows the ulcer on her anus.

MY LITTLE LOVELIES

A tearful tincture washes
Cabbage-green skies;
Beneath the dribbling bushes
Your raincoats lie;

Pale white in private moonlight,
Like round-eyed sores,
Flap your scabby kneecaps apart,
My ugly whores!

We loved each other in those days,
Ugly blue whore!
We ate boiled eggs
And weed.

One night you made me a poet,
Ugly blond whore.
Get between my legs,
I'll whip you.

I puked up your greasy hair,
Ugly black whore;
You tried to unstring
My guitar.

Blah! Some of my dried-up spit,
Ugly red whore,
Still stinks in the cracks
Of your breast.

O my little lovelies,
I hate your guts!
Go stick big blisters
On your ugly tits!

Break the cracked bottles and jars
Of my feelings;
Come on! Be my ballerinas
Just for a while!

Your shoulderblades are twisted back,
My masterpieces!
Stick stars in your snatches and shake
Them to bits!

And it was for you hunks of meat
I wrote my rhymes!
My love was sticky self-deceit
And dirty games!

Dumb bunch of burnt-out stars,
– Against the walls!
Go back to God, croak in corners
Like animals!

Shining in private moonlight
Like round-eyed sores,
Flap your scabby kneecaps apart,
My ugly whores!

THE SISTERS OF CHARITY

This youth, his brilliant eye and shining skin,
His perfect body and his twenty years, should go
Unclothed, and some strange Genie in a copper crown
Have loved him, in Persia, by moonlight, long ago.

Impetuous youth, dark virginal delights;
His first intoxication spins in his head
Like newborn seas, the tears of summer nights
That turn forever in their diamond bed.

The youth before the squalor of this world
Feels his heart moved with a profound ire –
Pierced with the deep eternal wound,
His Sister of Charity is all his desire.

But Woman, unbridled heap of organs, soft care,
You are never our Sister of Charity, no,
Not in dark looks, nor the belly's sleeping shade,
Nor small fingers, nor breasts more splendid than snow.

Slumbering blindness with enormous eyes,
All our embrace is but a single question:
For you, breast-bearer, have recourse to us;
We cradle you, delightful grave affection.

Your hate, your set torpors, your weaknesses,
    your spite,
All the brutalities you suffered long ago,
You return to us, all without evil, O Night,
In an excess of blood that every month will flow.

Woman, carried away, an instant appalls him
With love, the call of life and song of action –
Then the bitter Muse and burning Justice call him,
To dismember him with their august obsession.

Ah! Ceaselessly thirsting after splendors and calms,
Forsaken by the relentless Sisters, he moans
Softly for the knowledge that comes in open arms,
And toward bright nature bears a forehead stained
    with blood.

But obscure alchemy and the occult sciences
Repulse the wounded youth, dark scholar of his pride;
A savage solitude rolls over him.
Then beautiful still, disdainful of the grave,

Let him believe in vast goals, Voyages and Dreams
Endless and immense, across dark midnights of Truth,
And summon you to soothe his soul and fevered limbs,
O Sister of Charity, O Mystery, O Death.

THE LADIES WHO LOOK FOR LICE

When the child's forehead, red and full of pain,
Dreams of ease in the streaming of white veils,
To the side of his bed two lovely sisters come
With delicate fingers and long silvery nails.

They take the child with them to an immense
Window, where blue air bathes a flowery grove,
And through his heavy hair, as the dew descends,
Their terrible, enchanting fingers probe.

He listens to their fearful slow breath vibrate,
Flowering with honey and the hue of roses,
Broken now and then with whispers, saliva
Licked back on their lips, a longing for kisses.

He hears their lashes beat the still, sweet air;
Their soft electric fingers never tire –
Through his gray swoon, a crackling in his hair –
Beneath their royal nails the little lice expire.

Within him then surges the wine of Idleness,
Like the sweet deluding harmonica's sigh;
And the child can feel, beneath their slow caresses,
Rising, falling, an endless desire to cry.

SEVEN-YEAR-OLD POETS

The Mother closed the copybook, and went away
Content, and very proud, and never saw
In the blue eyes, beneath the pimply forehead,
The horror and loathing in her child's soul.

All day he sweat obedience; was very
Bright; still, some black tics, some traits he had
Seemed to foreshadow sour hypocrisies.
In the dark halls, their mildewed paper peeling,
He passed, stuck out his tongue, then pressed two fists
In his crotch, and shut his eyes to see spots.
A door opened: in the evening lamplight
There he was, gasping on the banisters
In a well of light that hung beneath the roof.
Summer especially, stupid, slow, he always tried
To shut himself up in the cool latrine:
There he could think, be calm, and sniff the air.

Washed from the smells of day, the garden, in winter,
Out behind the house, filled with moonlight;
Stretched below a wall, and rolled in dirt,
Squeezing his dazzled eyes to make visions come,
He only heard the scruffy fruit trees grow.
A pity! The friends he had were puny kids,
The ones with runny eyes that streaked their cheeks,

Who hid thin yellow fingers, smeared with mud,
Beneath old cast-off clothes that stank of shit;
They used to talk like gentle idiots.
If she surprised him in these filthy friendships
His mother grew afraid; the child's deep tenderness
Took her astonishment to task. How good . . .
Her wide blue eyes – but they lie.

Seven years old; he made up novels: life
In the desert, Liberty in transports gleaming,
Forests, suns, shores, swamps! Inspiration
In picture magazines: he looked, red-faced,
At Spanish and Italian girls who laughed.
And when, with brown eyes, wild, in calico,
– She was eight – the workers' girl next door
Played rough, jumped right on top of him
In a corner, onto his back, and pulled his hair,
And he was under her, he bit her ass
Because she wore no panties underneath;
Then, beaten by her, hit with fists and heels,
He took the smell of her skin back to his room.

He hated pale December Sunday afternoons:
With plastered hair, on a mahogany couch,
He read the cabbage-colored pages of a Bible;
Dreams oppressed him every night in bed.
He hated God, but loved the men he saw

Returning home in dirty working clothes
Through the wild evening air to the edge of town,
Where criers, rolling drums before the edicts,
Made the crowds around them groan and laugh.
– He dreamed of prairies of love, where shining herds,
Perfumes of life, pubescent stalks of gold
Swirled slowly round, and then rose up and flew.

The darkest things in life could move him most;
When in that empty room, the shutters closed,
High and blue, with its bitter humid smell,
He read his novel – always on his mind –
Full of heavy ocher skies and drowning forests,
Flowers of flesh in starry woods uncurled,
Catastrophe, vertigo, pity and disaster!
– While the noises of the neighborhood swelled
Below – stretched out alone on unbleached
Canvas sheets, a turbulent vision of sails!

FIRST COMMUNIONS

I

They're ugly, those churches in country towns
Where fifteen stupid kids smear up the wall
And listen to an ugly priest as he drones
Away – his shoes and rotting stockings smell –
But through leafy branches the sun shines
In the old colors of the crude stained glass.

The stone always smells of the soil outside.
You see those piles of boulders that retain
The solemn motion of the rutting countryside,
Divide the ripening wheat from yellow lanes,
Support blue plums in trees the sun has dried,
Black knots of mulberries, and sticky vines.

Those barns have stood untouched for centuries;
Their dark interiors are cold and dank.
The walls are hung with grotesque mysteries –
Our Lady, or a martyr's bloody flanks –
Still, stinking stable flies and kitchen flies
Devour old wax spilt on the sun-stained planks.

'The child's first duty of course is to the home,
To family cares and good back-breaking work ...'
They leave, forgetting that their faces burn
Where the Priest of Christ has given them a smack.
– He lets them out at harvesttime, thus earns
His little house with three shade trees in back.

Their first long pants, a perfect day for pastry,
Napoleon, or *The Drummer Boy*, above
An engraving where the Holy Family
Sticks out their tongues in a surfeit of love –
Joined by two maps in an Age of Industry –
These memories of the Great Day are all they have.

The girls would always go to church, content
To hear themselves called bitches by the boys
After Mass, or after vespers during Lent.
The boys, who'll end up stationed overseas,
Disturb decorum in the cafés they frequent
With shouts, with dirty songs, and brand-new clothes.

Yet the Pastor picked out holy pictures
For youngsters; in his room on Saturday night
He heard the distant dances; the strictures
Of heaven crumble, his toes tap with delight
As he reveled in Night's benedictions –
Night, black pirate on a sea of golden light.

II

Among the catechists the Priest recognized
(Not from the better part of town) one child,
An unknown little girl, with large sad eyes
And sallow skin. Her parents seemed poor, and old.
'On the Great Day, choosing her as His prize,
God will rain His choicest blessings on this child.'

III

The day before the Great Day, she fell ill.
Like whispering in the church, dark and high,
She felt a shivering she could not still,
An endless shivering: 'I am going to die.'

Forgiving her stupid sisters' trespasses,
She lay exhausted, and through her head poured
Streams of angels, Virgins, Jesuses,
And, tranquilly, her soul drank down the Lord.

Adonai! A shower of Latin lines,
Green watery clouds, caress her fevered eyes,
And stained with blood in heavenly designs,
Great white linens fall across the skies!

For her virginity – present and to come –
She bites the ice of your Remission.
Yet more than water lilies, more than sweet desserts,
Your forgiveness is frigid, Queen of Sion!

IV

But Our Lady is only a lady in prayerbooks,
And mystic exaltations sometimes fail.
Then pictures grow dark, and bored looks
Lacquer them; engravings grow dim; prints pale.

And then an immodest desire to peek
Startles shining sky-blue dreams of the Good,
Frantic to undo that celestial coat
Whose linen hides the nakedness of God.

She tries, ah, still she tries, her soul distressed
And her face in a pillow, stifling sobs,
To prolong those streaks of aching tenderness,
And drools ... and shadows fill the house and yard.

The child can stand no more. She turns upon
Her back and pulls the curtains loose
To feel the freshness of the air pour in
Beneath the sheet, onto her burning breast ...

V

She woke at midnight: white was the window
Beyond the blue slumber of the moon-soaked shade,
Drenched in visions of white veils on Sunday;
She had dreamed red. Her nose bled,

And to enjoy in God, though weak and chaste,
Her burgeoning love, she thirsted after night,
When the heart, beneath the tender gaze
Of heaven, falls and rises in delight;

Night, Virgin Mother impalpable, who bathes
All childish raptures in soft gray surcease;
Thirsted after night, when a bleeding heart
Releases stifled rebellion in peace.

Thus become both Victim and the child bride,
Candle in hand, beneath her star she flees
To the courtyard where a shirt still hung to dry,
White ghost, and raises black ghosts in the trees.

VI

She passed her holy vigil in the outhouse.
Around her small candle swirled the white air,
Moving a wild vine with a purplish gloss
That twisted through a wall in disrepair.

The skylight lit the courtyard; in the east
The sky plated windows with red-gold streams
Of light; the pavement smelled of watery bleach
Beneath sulfurous walls that dripped dark dreams.

VII

Who will describe these filthy agonies,
And the hate that awaits her, you mad priests
Whose divine labor still warps the world,
When leprosy upon her body feasts?

VIII

When she has knotted up her hysterias
And sees through the dolors of happiness
Her lover dream of white millions of Marys,
The morning after love, then, in sadness:

'Do you know I have destroyed you? Turned your head,
And taken your heart, your life, and your dreams;
I am sick: Oh, lay me down among the Dead
Whose thirst is quenched by dark nocturnal streams!

'For I was young, and Christ has soured my soul.
He filled me to the throat with sick disgust!
You kissed my hair, my hair as thick as wool,
And I lay and let you ... Ah, you love your lust,

'You Men! You little think the woman most in love,
Ruled by a conscience full of sordid terror,
Is prostituted worse than any slave,
And that all our love for you is error!

'My First Communion is over and past.
I can never have understood your kisses:
For my soul and body embraced by your flesh
Crawled with the rotten kiss of Jesus!'

IX

So the festering soul, the soul disconsolate,
Will feel Your curses stream upon her head.
She will have made her bed in Your unsoiled Hate,
And left true passion for an image of death,

Christ! O Christ, eternal thief of energy!
God crucified, whose pallor feeds on women
Nailed to the ground with shame and with migraine,
Or else thrown down upon their backs, in pain.

'THE SAVIOR BUMPED UPON HIS HEAVY BUTT'

The Savior bumped upon his heavy butt,
A ray of light across his shoulder; I sweat,
Begin to shout: 'You want to see the sky turn red?
You hanging there waiting for the roar of floods,
For milk-white stars, and swarms of asteroids?

'Your forehead is spiky from your midnight games,
Savior! Come on in out of the rain! And pray –
For a sheet on your mealy mouth to shut you up!
If some lost traveler bumps into your grave, just say:
Brother, move on, I'm crippled and I can't get up!'

But the Savior kept hanging, open-mouthed with fear,
As lawns turn bluish when the sun has died:
'Listen, will you sell your knees as souvenirs?
Old Abraham! Big Pilgrim! Sniveler of psalms!
Velvet glove! Watering Mount Olivet with tears!

'A bore at home, nothing but trouble in town!
Heart among flowers; pious and oh, so sweet!
Love and blindness! Majesty! Virtuous renown,
Savior! Stupid, hot-eyed as a bitch in heat!
I'm the soul in agony! This passion is mine!

'Stupid! I cry, my tears fall down like rain,
And still I laugh at the hope of your favor!
You know I am accursed! And drunk, and pale, insane,
You name it, anything! But go lie down, Savior,
Go lie down. I do not need your sluggish brain.

'You're it! The Savior! Fulfillment of all our hopes!
And still your calm reason and your saintly schemes
Whistle in the night like whales;
You get yourself hung up, and reel off requiems
On broken organs full of reedy stops!

'Behold the son of God! Coward! And if the cold
Heels of the divine feet trampled on my shoulders,
I'd call you coward still! That fly-specked forehead!
Socrates, Jesus: righteous both! Stupid Saviors!
Respect me, Accursed forever in nights of blood!

'Oh, make him go away, with his tonsils tied
Tightly in a scarf of shame, sweet as sugar
On a rotten tooth, sucking my boredom, satisfied –
Like a bitch who's just been jumped by horny doggies
Licks a piece of entrail dangling from her side.

'Forget your filthy charities, you hypocrite;
I hate the look in your runny rag-doll eyes!
Whining for papa like a snot-nosed kid,
An idiot waiting for music from on high!
Savior, your statuary gut is full of shit!'

I cried all this across the face of earth; night,
Calm and pale, as I raved, filled up the skies.
I looked: but the phantom had vanished from sight,
And carried from my lips these awful ironies.
Come, winds of darkness, visit the Accursed! Let light

Fall still across the azure palings of the sky,
While Order, eternal watchman, slowly sails
Among the whirling spaces of the Universe,
Enormous, eventless motion, and his net trails
In a luminous river of fiery stars.

'WHAT DO WE CARE, MY HEART'

What do we care, my heart, for streams of blood
And fire, a thousand murders, endless screams
Of anger, sobs of hell, order destroyed in a flood
Of fire, as over all the North Wind streams:

Vengeance entire? Nothing! Oh, yes, entire!
Captains of Industry, Princes, perish! This we desire!
Power, Justice, History, fall! Down with the old!
You owe us that. Blood! Blood! And flames of gold!

Dream on of war, of vengeances and terrors,
My soul! Though we writhe in these teeth: Ah! Fall,
Republics of this world! Emperors,
Regiments, Colonies, Nations, all!

Who will stir up whirlwinds of furious fire
If we do not, and those whom we call brothers?
Join us, Romantic friends! Forget all others!
And never will we work, O waves of fire!

Europe, Asia, America, vanish!
Our avenging advance has ravished and sacked
Towns and countryside! We will be punished!
Volcanoes will explode! And Ocean attacked . . .

Oh, friends! Be calm, these are brothers, my heart:
Dark strangers, suppose we begin! Let's go, let's go!
Disaster! I tremble, the old earth,
On me, and yours, ah, more and more! The earth
    dissolves.

It's nothing; I'm here – I'm still here.

THE STOLEN HEART

My weeping heart on the deck drools spit;
They soil it with cigarette butts,
They spatter it with slop and shit;
My weeping heart on the deck drools spit.
The soldiers drink and laugh at it;
The sound of laughing hurts my guts.
My weeping heart on the deck drools spit;
They soil it with cigarette butts.

Soldiers' cocks are a black burlesque;
They rape my heart with what they say.
In scrawls on the mast, grotesque
Soldiers' cocks are a black burlesque.
Ocean, abracadabrantesque,
Take my heart and wash it away!
Soldiers' cocks are a black burlesque;
They rape my heart with what they say.

When they are done, and all worn out
How will I act, my stolen heart?
All I will hear is a drunken shout
When they are done and all worn out.
I will throw up and then pass out,
I know, with my heart torn apart
When they are done, and all worn out.
How will I act, my stolen heart?

THE DRUNKEN BOAT

I drifted on a river I could not control,
No longer guided by the bargemen's ropes.
They were captured by howling Indians
Who nailed them naked to colored stakes.

I cared no more for other boats or cargoes:
English cotton, Flemish wheat, all were gone.
When my bargemen could no longer haul me
I forgot about everything and drifted on.

Through the wild splash and surging of the tides
Last winter, deaf as a child's dark night,
I ran and ran! And the drifting Peninsulas
Have never known such conquering delight.

Lighter than cork, I revolved upon waves
That roll the dead forever in the deep,
Ten days, beyond the blinking eyes of land!
Lulled by storms, I drifted seaward from sleep.

Sweeter than children find the taste of sour fruit,
Green water filled my cockle shell of pine.
Anchor and rudder went drifting away,
Washed in vomit and stained with blue wine.

Now I drift through the Poem of the Sea;
This gruel of stars mirrors the milky sky,
Devours green azures; ecstatic flotsam,
Drowned men, pale and thoughtful, sometimes drift by.

Staining the sudden blueness, the slow sounds,
Deliriums that streak the glowing sky,
Stronger than drink and the songs we sing,
It is boiling, bitter, red; it is love!

I watched the lightning tear the sky apart,
Watched waterspouts, and streaming undertow,
And Dawn like Dove-People rising on wings –
I've seen what men have only dreamed they saw!

I saw the sun with mystic horrors darken
And shimmer through a violet haze;
With a shiver of shutters the waves fell
Like actors in ancient, forgotten plays!

I dreamed of green nights and glittering snow,
Slow kisses rising in the eyes of the Sea,
Unknown liquids flowing, the blue and yellow
Stirring of phosphorescent melody!

For months I watched the surge of the sea,
Hysterical herds attacking the reefs;
I never thought the bright feet of Mary
Could muzzle up the heavy-breathing waves!

I have jostled – you know? – unbelievable Floridas
And seen among the flowers the wild eyes
Of panthers in the skins of men! Rainbows
Bridling blind flocks beneath the horizons!

In stinking swamps I have seen great hulks:
A Leviathan that rotted in the reeds!
Water crumbling in the midst of calm
And distances that shatter into foam.

Glaciers, silver suns, waves of pearl, fiery skies,
Giant serpents stranded where lice consume
Them, falling in the depths of dark gulfs
From twisted trees, bathed in black perfume!

I wanted to show children these fishes shining
In the blue wave, the golden fish that sing –
A froth of flowers cradled my wandering
And delicate winds tossed me on their wings.

Sometimes, a martyr of poles and latitudes,
The sea rocked me softly in sighing air,
And brought me shadow-flowers with yellow stems –
I remained like a woman, kneeling ...

Almost an island, I balanced on my boat's sides
Rapacious blond-eyed birds, their dung, their screams.
I drifted on. Through fragile tangled lines
Drowned men, still staring up, sank down to sleep.

Now I, a little lost boat, in swirling debris,
Tossed by the storm into the birdless upper air
– All the Hansa Merchants and Monitors
Could not fish up my body drunk with the sea;

Free and soaring, trailing a violet haze,
Shot through the sky, a reddening wall
Wet with the jam of poets' inspiration,
Lichens of sun, and snots of bright blue sky;

Lost branch spinning in a herd of hippocamps,
Covered over with electric animals,
An everlasting July battering
The glittering sky and its fiery funnels;

Shaking at the sound of monsters roaring,
Rutting Behemoths in thick whirlpools,
Eternal weaver of unmoving blues,
I thought of Europe and its ancient walls!

I have seen archipelagos in the stars,
Feverish skies where I was free to roam!
Are these bottomless nights your exiled nests,
Swarm of golden birds, O Strength to come?

True, I've cried too much; I am heartsick at dawn.
The moon is bitter and the sun is sour ...
Love burns me; I am swollen and slow.
Let my keel break! Oh, let me sink in the sea!

If I long for a shore in Europe,
It's a small pond, dark, cold, remote,
The odor of evening, and a child full of sorrow
Who stoops to launch a crumpled paper boat.

Washed in your languors, Sea, I cannot trace
The wake of tankers foaming through the cold,
Nor assault the pride of pennants and flags,
Nor endure the slave ship's stinking hold.

VOWELS

Black A, white E, red I, green U, blue O – vowels,
Some day I will open your silent pregnancies:
A, black belt, hairy with burst flies,
Bumbling and buzzing over stinking cruelties,

Pits of night; E, candor of sand and pavilions,
High glacial spears, white kings, trembling Queen
　　Anne's lace;
I, bloody spittle, laughter dribbling from a face
In wild denial or in anger, vermilions;

U, ... divine movement of viridian seas,
Peace of pastures animal-strewn, peace of calm lines
Drawn on foreheads worn with heavy alchemies;

O, supreme Trumpet, harsh with strange stridencies,
Silences traced in angels and astral designs:
O ... OMEGA ... the violet light of His Eyes!

'THE SUN HAS WEPT ROSE'

The sun has wept rose in the shell of your ears,
The world has rolled white from your back, your
    thighs;
The sea has stained rust the crimson of your breasts,
And Man has bled black at your sovereign side.

Stupra: THREE SCATOLOGICAL SONNETS

'ANIMALS ONCE SPEWED SEMEN'

Animals once spewed semen as they ran,
Their organs streaked with blood and excrement.
Our fathers pouched their members out, and spent
Long hours contriving to display their span.

The medieval woman, saint or whore,
Asked for a gallant with a proud display;
Even Kléber, to look at his pants (they
Lie, perhaps, somewhat), had resource, and more.

Man and the proudest mammals have one source;
Their giant cocks and ours are both the same . . .
And yet a sterile hour now sounds; the horse

And roaring bull have covered up their flame;
No one dares undo his genital force
In those woods where sex was once a children's
    game . . .

'OUR ASSHOLES ARE DIFFERENT'

Our assholes are different from theirs. I used to watch
Young men let down their pants behind some tree,
And in those happy floods that youth set free
I watched the architecture of our crotch.

Quite firm, in many cases pale, it owes
Its form to muscles, and a wickerwork
Of hairs; for girls, the most enchanting lurk
In a dark crack where tufted satin grows.

The touching and wonderful innocence
Of painted cherubs on a Baroque shrine
Is recalled in that cheek a dimple indents ...

Oh! If only we were naked now, and free
To watch our protruding parts align;
To whisper – both of us – in ecstasy!

'HIDDEN AND WRINKLED'

Hidden and wrinkled like a budding violet
It breathes, gently worn out, in a tangled vine
(Still damp with love), on the soft incline
Of white buttocks to the rim of the pit.

Thin streams like rivers of milk; innocent
Tears, shed beneath hot breath that drives them down
Across small clots of rich soil, reddish brown,
Where they lose themselves in the dark descent . . .

My mouth always dribbles with its coupling force;
My soul, jealous of the body's intercourse,
Makes it a tearful, wild necessity.

Ecstatic olive branch, the flute one blows,
The tube where heavenly praline flows,
Promised Land in sticky femininity.

'O SEASONS, O CHÂTEAUS!'

O seasons, O châteaus!
Where is the flawless soul?

O seasons, O châteaus,

I learned the magic of
Felicity. It enchants us all.

Long live Felicity, when
Gaul's cock crows!

Now all desire has gone;
It has made my life its own.

That spell! It caught my heart and soul
And scattered every trial.

What is the meaning of all I say?
It blows my words away!

O seasons, O châteaus!

REMEMBRANCE

I

Water, clear as the salt of children's tears.
Suddenly in sunlight, women's bodies, all white;
Streams of silk, pure lilies, bright banners
Beneath ramparts where an armed Maid appeared.

Diversion of angels; No – the current carries gold
And loads its heavy, black, cool arms with grass,
Sinking beneath its canopy of sky . . . and the arch
And shadows of the hill, like curtains, unfold.

II

Watch! This wet square of stream moves in soft swirls,
In endless glassy gold pavilioning its bed;
Like willow trees where birds hop unhindered
Are the green gauzy dresses of the little girls.

Flowers brighter than coin, warm yellow eyes
That trouble waters – O Wife, your conjugal love! –
The rosy Sun at noon burns sullenly above
This dark mirror, reflected through hazy skies.

III

MADAME in the open field stands too straight
In a swirl of snowy threads, her parasol
Unsheathed; she snaps flower tops to watch
   them fall ...
Her children read their red-backed book, and wait,

Wait, in the flowering grass. Alas! HE
Like a thousand bright angels scattering in flight
Scales the mountaintops and fades from sight!
Behind him runs the black, unbending SHE!

IV

Regret for the thick young arms of virgin grass!
Gold of April moonlight in the sacred bed! Joy
Of abandoned boat docks on the riverbank, prey
To the August nights that bred this rottenness!

Now let her weep beneath these walls! The breath
Of towering poplars is the only breeze.
And then this water, sourceless, somber, gray,
And a man who drags the bottom in a motionless
   barge.

V

Toy for this dull eye of water, I cannot reach
– O motionless boat! Too short, my arms! –
These flowers: the yellow one that bothers me
There, nor the blue, friend to water the color of ash!

From wing-shaken willows a powder drifts;
The roses in the reeds have long since dried.
My boat, still motionless; and its chain pulled
Deep in this edgeless eye of water ... into what mud?

TEAR

Far from flocks, from birds and country girls,
I knelt down to drink within a leafy screen
Surrounded by tender hazelnut trees
In the warm green mist of afternoon.

What could I drink from this young Oise,
Tongueless trees, flowerless grass, dark skies . . .
What could I draw from the round gourd that
     grew there?
Some tasteless golden draught to make me sweat.

And a poor sign for an inn would I have made.
Later, toward evening, the sky filled with storms . . .
They became black fields, and lakes, and poles of wood,
Tunnels within the blue night, and waiting rooms.

Water from the woods runs out on virgin sands,
The wind from heaven casts ice thick on the ponds . . .
Now, like one who dives for pretty shells or coin,
Never deny that my thirst has caused me pain!

THE COMEDY OF THIRST

I. FOREFATHERS

We are your Father's Fathers,
      Your Elders!
Glistening with the cold sweat
Of the moon and dripping leaves.
... But our dry wines were strong!
Beneath this guileless sun
What is the duty of man? To drink.

I: To die by untamed streams.

    We are your Father's Fathers,
      Villagers.
Water murmurs in the reeds:
See where the swirling moat
Circles the sweating château.
Come down with us to the cellars
And you shall have cider and milk.

I: Let us go with the cattle to drink.
    We are your Father's Fathers,
      Preservers

Of liquors in cabinets;
Teas! and Coffees! so rare,
Tremble in our stills.
... Look at these forms and flowers.
We have come from the graveyard.

I: Ah! If I could empty all the urns ...

II. THE SPIRIT

Eternal water sprites,
Part the pure waters;
Venus, foam-born,
Dazzle the bright wave.

Wandering Jews of Norway,
Say the snow to me;
Dear age-old exiles,
Tell me the sea.

Forget these pure liquids,
These waterflowers for cups;
No legends, no figures
Can soften my thirst.

Songmaker, see your godchild –
My wild desire to drink,
The headless Hydra in my bowels
That feeds upon my soul.

III. FRIENDS

Come, all Wines go down to the sea,
In inexhaustible waves!
See the foaming Bitter Beer
Pour from mountain caves!

Knowing pilgrims, seek repose
By the emerald pillars of Absinthe . . .

I: Leave these landscapes.
    Friends, what is drunkenness?

    I would as soon lie dumb
    To fester in some pond
    Beneath the stinking scum
    By a drifting log.

IV. THE POOR MAN DREAMS

I have an evening unspent
When I can drink in peace
In a small quiet place,
And then die content . . .
Since I am patient.

If I forget my pain,
If I can get some gold,
Should I live in the North
Or in the wine-blest South?
. . . Ah, dreaming is vain

Since it's always a loss!
And if I become once more
The wanderer I was,
The doors of the green inn
Can never be opened again.

V. CONCLUSION

The pigeons trembling in the open field,
The wild running things that see the night,
Waterbugs and lap dogs, and the wild
And silly butterfly – alike, all thirst!

Oh, but to vanish like the trackless cloud!
Wrapped in wetness and in dew, to die
Among the violets on the waterside
Daylight leaves in heaps about the wood.

'HEAR HOW IT BELLOWS'

Hear how it bellows
Beneath the acacias
In April, the green
Branch of the vine!

In a cleansing cloud
To Phoebe! See them nod
And turn a head
Like saints of old . . .

Far from shining stones
On capes, from bright roofs,
Dear Ancients desire
This sullen syrup . . .

Never festive, not
Astral, the misty
Breath of this
Nocturnal scene.

Yet still they stay
. . . Germany, Sicily,
In this sad pale
Mist, and justly.

LOVELY THOUGHTS FOR MORNING

At four in the morning, in summertime,
Love's drowsiness still lasts.
Dawn brushes from the shrubbery
    The odor of the night's feast.

Beyond the bright Hesperides,
Within the western workshop of the Sun,
Carpenters in shirtsleeves scramble;
    Work is begun.

And in desolate, moss-grown isles
They carve precious panels
Where the wealth of cities laughs
    Beneath a hollow sky.

For these charming dabblers in the arts
Who labor for a king in Babylon,
Venus! Leave for a moment
    Lovers' haloed hearts.

    O Queen of Shepherds!
Carry the purest eau-de-vie
To these workmen while they rest
And take their bath at noonday, in the sea.

MICHAEL AND CHRISTINE

Damn, Damn! Suppose the sun leaves these shores!
Blow on, bright storm! There's the shadow of the
   highway.
In the willows, in the old courtyard,
The storm first spatters in the dusty clay.

O flock of lambs, blond soldiers of our idyll,
Flee from these fountains, this spindly thicket!
Now plain and desert, horizon and field
Are still before the reddening storm's toilette.

Black dog, brown shepherd muffled in a cloak,
Flee the towering lightnings of the storm;
Blond flock, scurry through the sulfury dark,
Go and huddle someplace deep and warm.

Yet I, Lord God! See how my soul
Soars into skies frozen with red,
In heavenly clouds that whirl and roll
Above Solognes long as a railroad.

See the thousand wolves, the thousand wild seeds
Borne upon the storm, on this religious afternoon
That loves the weeds and scatters them
Across old Europe where a hundred hordes ride!

Afterward, moonlight! Warriors, over the plain,
Redden their faces in the darkened skies
And gallop their great pale horses away!
The pebbles beneath them spatter like rain!

And we see the yellow wood and the valley of light,
The blue-eyed Bride, the red-faced Gaul, and
The white Pascal Lamb, at their delicate feet,
Michael and Christine – and Christ! The idyll's end.

THE RIVER OF CORDIAL

The River of Cordial rolls ignored
       In empty countryside:
Lulled by the voices of a hundred
       Crows, a celestial tide,
And great pine branches overhead
       That the wild winds ride.

All things roll here: horrors of midnights,
       Campaigns of a lost year,
Dungeons disturbed, and groves of lights;
       Echoing on these shores, still clear,
Dead ecstasies of questing knights –
       Yet how the wind revives us here!

The wanderer who watches these black bands
       Takes courage as he goes;
Forest soldiers that the Lord commands,
       Dear, delightful crows!
Chase the crafty peasant from these lands,
       And the old claw he shows.

THE TRIUMPH OF PATIENCE

In the bright branches of the willow trees
The echo of a hunt dissolves,
But elegant songs still beat the air
Among the trembling leaves.
Let our blood laugh in our veins.
This place is a tangle of vines;
The sky has an angel's face.
Air and water are one and the same.
I shall go out. If bright light wounds me
I shall lie down on leaves and die.

To wait, to be bored, is too simple;
All my anguish is empty.
Let high summer dangle me
Behind its fatal glittering car.
O Nature, let me die in you
... Less useless, less alone ...
Not like the Shepherds, who will die
More or less throughout the world.

Let turning seasons do their worst;
To you, Nature, I offer up myself,
My hunger and my everlasting thirst;
To quiet them I ask your help.
Nothing at all can ever deceive me;
We laugh with our parents when we laugh in the sun,
But I will laugh with nothing, with no one;
And I will be free in this misfortune.

A SONG FROM THE HIGHEST TOWER

Idle children
Held in thrall,
Lack of heart
Has cost my life.
Oh, will the day come
When all hearts fall in love?

Leave and go hide,
To myself I cry:
There is no promise
Of a greater joy.
Let nothing prevent
My high retreat.

I have waited so long
That at length I forget,
And leave unto heaven
My fear and regret;
A sick thirst
Darkens my veins.

So the green field
To oblivion falls,
Overgrown, flowering
With incense and weeds
And the cruel noise
Of dirty flies.

Ah! Widowed again and again,
The poor soul
Who has only a picture
Of the Mother of God!
Can one really pray
To the Virgin Mary?

Idle children
Held in thrall,
Lack of heart
Has cost my life.

Oh, will the day come
When all hearts fall in love?

ETERNITY

It is recovered.
Why? Eternity.
In the whirling light
Of sun become sea.

O my sentinel soul,
Let us desire
The nothing of night
And the day on fire.

From the applause of the World
And the striving of Man
You set yourself free
And fly as you can.

For out of you only,
Soft silken embers,
Duty arises
Nor surfeit remembers.

Then shall all hope fail,
No *orietur*.
Science with patience,
The torment is sure.

It is recovered.
What? Eternity.
In the whirling light
Of sun become sea.

GOLDEN AGE

One of these voices
– Angelically –
Greenly, angrily,
Talks about me.

These thousands of questions
That spread themselves out
Can lead to nothing
But madness and rout;

Remember this tune
So gentle and free:
This flowering wave
Is your own family!

And then the voice sings. Oh
So gently, so free,
And I join the song
For all to see ...

Remember this tune
So gentle and free:
This flowering wave
Is your own family! ... etc. ...

And then a new voice
– How angelically! –
Greenly, angrily,
Talks about me:

And it sings just then,
A sister of the winds;
In a German accent,
But passionately –

The world is evil;
Does that surprise you?
Live; to the fire
Leave his obscure pain.

O lovely château!
O life full of light!
To what Age do you belong,
Our older brother's
Princely soul? etc. . . .

I have my song too,
Several sisters! Voices
Not to be heard!
Enfold me
In your bashful light . . . etc. . . .

THE NEWLYWEDS AT HOME

The bedroom lies open to the turquoise sky;
No room; nothing but boxes and bins!
The wall without is full of wild flowers
And quivers with goblins' chattering gums!

How like the intrigues of genies is this:
All this expense and these vain disorders!
There is an African fairy who provides
The mulberry and cobwebs in the corners!

Enter severally, disgruntled godmothers
As spots of light upon the wainscoting.
The household departs (but not these others!)
In a lightheaded rush, and nothing gets done . . .

Every husband has a wind (here it blows
All day long) that cheats him unawares . . .
Even wicked fairies from the water
Come to flutter in the alcove's affairs.

The night, the friendly night – oh! the honeymoon
Will snatch away their smile and fill the sky
With a thousand copper coronets!
They will deal with a bad rat by and by.

If a wandering light doesn't happen along
Like a rifle shot just after evensong . . .
Holy white specters of Bethlehem . . . oh!
Enchant instead the sky in their window!

BRUSSELS
July   Regent's Boulevard

Flower beds of amaranths up to
The pleasant palace of Jupiter.
You I know spread here your Blue,
Your desert Blue, almost-Sahara Blue!

Roses here and sunlit pines
Play convoluted games with vines,
Cages in a little widow's window . . .
What bands of birds! Oh! ah! oh! ah! oh!

Quiet houses, love calmed long ago!
Kiosk for a Woman Mad with Regret!
Behind the butts of rose trees, low
And shadowy, a balcony for Juliet . . .

. . . Say Juliet, I think of Henriette,
A lovely stop along the railway,
Where in a mountain, at an orchard's end,
A thousand blue devils dance a ballet!

On a green bench in a hurricane cloud
The white girl of Ireland sings to her guitar;
In the Guianan dining room, loud
Sounds of children, where the birdcages are.

Ducal Window makes me think of subtile
Poison slugs and snails, and here below
Asleep in sunshine, boxwood hedge ... but oh,
It is all too beautiful! Let us be still.

Calm boulevard, empty of life and fire!
Tragedy, Comedy, all in stillness stands;
Infinite imagination here expands,
And I who know you quietly admire.

'DOES SHE DANCE?'

Does she dance? In the first blue hours
Will she wither like the dying flowers . . .
Before this sweep of splendor perfumed
By the flowering breath of the bustling town!

It's all too beautiful! But necessary . . .
For the Fishermaid and the Pirate's song,
And for those masks who linger on
To feast at night upon the pure sea!

THE TRIUMPH OF HUNGER

Hunger, hunger, sister Anne,
Leave me if you can.

I only find within my bones
A taste for eating earth and stones.
Dinn! Dinn! Dinn! Dinn! We eat air,
Rocks and coals and iron ore.

My hunger, turn. Hunger, feed:
A field of bran.
Gather as you can the bright
Poison weed.

Eat the rocks a beggar breaks,
Stones of churches' crumbling gates,
Pebbles, children of the flood,
Loaves left lying in the mud.

Hunger, these are bits of black air,
    Cold clouds;
I follow as my stomach bids –
    And despair.

Across the land the leaves appear;
I seek the soft flesh of fruit.
In the heart of the furrow
I look for spring lettuce, and violets.

    Hunger, hunger, sister Anne,
    Leave me if you can.

SHAME

As long as a knife has not cut
This brain, unfolding
White wrapping, greasy, green,
Its odor always cold,

(He, this thing, should slit
His nose, lips, ears, belly, all!
Disown and leave his legs!
A marvel!)

No; I know that as long as
A knife has not cut his head
Nor a rock crushed his thigh
Nor fire seared his gut,

As long as none has acted, this child,
This bother, this mindless beast,
Will never for an instant rest
From trickery and treason,

And like a Rocky Mountain cat
Will stink in the world's air!
Yet when he dies, O God . . .
Let someone say a prayer.

CHILDHOOD

I

An idol ...
Black eyes, yellow hair;
Without parents or home,
Nobler than Flemish or Mexican fables;
His empire, in blues and insolent greens,
Spreads over beaches savagely named
In Greek, Celtic, or Slavic
By the shipless waves.

At the edge of the forest, where dream flowers chime,
Brighten and break ...
An orange-lipped girl, her knees crossed
In the bright flood that rolls from the fields;
Nudity covered, shadowed and clothed
By rainbows, flowers, and the sea.

Ladies tilting on terraces next to the sea.
Children and giants; superb black women in the
    gray-green moss,
Standing jewels in the shiny rich soil
Of groves and thawing gardens ...
Young mothers, older sisters, with a look of
    pilgrimages in their eyes;
Sultanas, princesses, dressed and walking like tyrants,
Foreign little girls, and people sweetly unhappy.

What a bore, all that talk about 'dear body' and
  'dear heart'!

II

There she is, the little girl, dead behind the rose trees.
The young mother, deceased, descends the steps.
Cousin's carriage squeaks on the sand.
Little brother (...but he's in India!) is there,
In a field of carnations, before the setting sun.
The old people, already buried, stand upright in a
  flowery wall.

A swarm of golden leaves surrounds the general's
  house;
They have gone south.
You follow the red road to come to the empty inn.
The château is for sale; its shutters hang loose.
The priest has probably gone away with the key to the
  church.
The keepers' lodges all about the park are uninhabited.
The fence of the park is so high
You can see only the rattling treetops beyond.
Besides, there is nothing to see inside.

The meadows lead off to villages empty of cocks,
Empty of anvils.
The floodgates are lifted. O crosses and windmills of
    the desert!
O islands and millstones ...

Magic flowers hummed. The slopes cradled him.
Animals of fabulous elegance wandered about.
Clouds gathered on high seas made of an eternity of
    scalding tears.

III

In the woods there is a bird;
His singing stops you, and you blush.

There is a clock that never strikes.

There is a little swamp, with a nest of pale animals.

There is a cathedral that sinks, and a lake that rises
    above it.

There is a little ribbon-covered cart, abandoned in the
    hedge
Or rolling away down the path.

There is a troupe of tiny strolling players all
    dressed up,
Seen on the road at the edge of the woods.

And when you are hungry or thirsty,
There is always someone to chase you away.

IV

I am a saint on a terrace praying –
Like gentle beasts who graze their way to the sea
    of Palestine.

I am a scholar in a dark armchair –
Branches and the rain beat at the casement of
    my library.

I am a highway walker in dwarf woods –
The rush of water in the sluices drown my steps.
My eyes are full of the sad golden wash of the sunset.

I might be an abandoned child,
Left on a causeway running into the sea;
A little lackey on a garden walk, that bumps against
    the sky.

The paths are bitter,
And broom flowers cover the hills.
The air is still ...
How far away are the birds and the fountains!
To go on can lead only to the end of the world.

V

Well, then, rent me a tomb, whitewashed and outlined
In cement ...
                    Far, far underground.

My elbows lean on the table, the lamp glares on
    newspapers
I am idiot enough to reread; on books without
    interest ...

At a great distance above my underground salon,
    the houses
Entrench themselves; fogs thicken ... mud is red
    or black.

                    Cancerous city ...
                    Night without end!

The sewers are not so high above me. On all sides,
The breadth of the globe.
Perhaps blue depths ... and wells of fire.
Moons in these dimensions may meet comets; the sea
    becomes myth.

In my bitter hours, I conjure up spheres of metal
    and sapphire.
I am Master of Silence.
But why should the appearance of an aperture
Gleam white in the corner of the vault?

TALE

A Prince was annoyed that he had forever devoted
    himself
Only to the perfection of vuglar generosities.
He foresaw astonishing revolutions in love,
And suspected that his wives were capable of more
Than an agreeable complacency,
Compounded of luxury and air.
He desired to see the Truth, the time of essential desire
And satisfaction.
Whether this would be an aberration of piety or no,
He desired it. And he possessed extensive human
    power.

All women who had known him were slaughtered.
What destruction in the garden of beauty!
Beneath the ax, they blessed him.
He ordered no new ones brought ... but women
    reappeared.
He killed all his followers, after the hunt,
Or his drinking bouts ...
But everyone followed him.
He amused himself by slaughtering rare animals.
He put the torch to his palaces.

He came down upon the people, and tore them
    to pieces ...
The crowd, the golden roofs, the beautiful beasts
Were still there.

Is ecstasy possible in destruction?
Can one grow young in cruelty?
The people made no sound. No one opposed his views.

He was riding one evening proudly alone, and a
    Genie appeared.
His beauty was ineffable ... even inexpressible.
In his face and his bearing shone the promise
Of a complex and many-layered love!
Of a happiness unbelievable, almost too much to bear,
The Prince and the Genie were lost in each other –
    disappearing, probably,
Into essential health.
How could they not have died of this?
Together then, they died.

But the Prince expired in his palace, at an ordinary
    age ...
The Prince was the Genie.
The Genie was the Prince.

    Our desire lacks the music of the mind.

PARADE

Strange, well-built young men.
Some of them have exploited *your* worlds.
They need nothing, and have little desire to put
    into play
Their splendid abilities and all that they know of
    your minds.
What sweet juicy strength!
Their eyes have the animal glaze of the summer night;
Red and black, tricolored,
The shine of steel stuck with stars of gold;
Their faces are warped, pitted, blemished, burned . . .
    The excesses of absolute madness –
    This cruel and tinseled stride!
Some of them are very young . . . (what would they
    think of Chérubin?) . . .
Equipped with frightening voices and several
    dangerous talents,
They are sent into town to take it from behind,
Tricked out with *disgusting* luxury.
A paradise of violence, of grimace and madness.
No comparison at all with your Fakirs
And your other entertainers on the stage.
Their suits are improvised in the taste of bad dreams;
They play lovesick songs, and tragic plays
Of buccaneers and demigods, wittier and cleverer

Than history or religion ever imagined.
Chinamen, Hottentots, Gypsies, Morons,
    Hyenas, Molochs,
Ancient insanities, sinister demons,
They distort popular maternal scenes
With bestial positions and caresses.
They play new plays and they sing the songs
Of the spinsters and the knitters in the sun . . .
Marvelous jugglers, with magnetic acting
They transfigure places and people.

Eyes flame, blood sings, bones begin to swell,
Tears start, and networks of scarlet ripple and throb.
Their jibes and their terror endure for a moment
Or can last for months upon end.

ONLY I HAVE THE KEY TO THIS SAVAGE PARADE!

ANTIQUE

Graceful son of Pan!
Around your forehead, circled with berries and flowers,
Your eyes, those glittering spheres, revolve.
Stained with the dregs of wine, your cheeks
Become hollow.

Your fangs gleam.
The curve of your breast is a lyre;
Tinklings vibrate in your blond arms.
Your heart beats in those loins
That cradle a double sex.
Wander about through the night,
Softly moving this thigh,
That second thigh . . .
And this leg,
The left . . .

BEING BEAUTEOUS

Against a fall of snow, a Being Beautiful, and very tall.
Whistlings of death and circles of faint music
    Make this adored body, swelling and trembling
        Like a specter, rise . . .
Black and scarlet gashes burst in the gleaming flesh.
The true colors of life grow dark,
                  Shimmer and separate
    In the scaffolding, around the Vision.

Shiverings mutter and rise,
    And the furious taste of these effects is charged
    With deadly whistlings and the raucous music
That the world, far behind us, hurls at our mother of
    beauty . . .
        She retreats, she rises up . . .
Oh! Our bones have put on new flesh, for love.

    O ash-white face

                  O tousled hair
    O crystal arms!

On this cannon I mean to destroy myself
        In a swirling of trees and soft air!

FAIRY

For Helen,
The ornamental saps conspired in the virgin dark;
In astral silences the trackless radiance unites.
The passion of summer is left to the tongueless birds,
And our necessary indolence tied
To a rich funeral barge in the eddying calm
Of dead loves and waning perfumes.

> After the moment of the foresters' song,
>   The rush of the torrent in wasted woods,
>   Cattle bells and echoes in the glen
>   And cries from the steppe ...

For Helen's childhood, hedges shivered, shadows
    trembled
(And the breast of the beggar, and the legends of
    Heaven).
Her eyes and her dancing, better far
Than priceless brilliance, cold influence,
Or the pleasures of the certain hour, the unique place.

VIGILS

I

This is a place of rest and light,
No fever, no longing,
In a bed or a field.

This is a friend, neither ardent nor weak. A friend.

This is my beloved, untormenting, untormented.
　My beloved.

Air, and a world all unlooked for. Life.
... Was it really this?
For the dream grows cold.

II

The lighting comes round to the roof-tree.
From opposite ends of the hall, nondescript
Harmonic elevations rise and meet.
The wall before the watcher
Is a succession of sections of friezes,
Atmospheric strata and geological faults.

A dream, swift and intense, of sentimental groups
Of beings in every character under every appearance.

III

The lamps and the carpets of my vigil
Make the sound of nocturnal waves,
Along the hull and all around the bottom deck.
This sea of my vigil, like Amelia's breasts.

Tapestries hung halfway up, a tangle of emerald lace,
And darting vigil doves . . .

At the back of the black hearth, real suns on seashores:
Ah! Wells of magic; this time, a single sight of dawn.

MYSTIQUE

On the side of the slope, angels revolving
Their dresses of wool, in fields of emerald and steel.

Flames shoot out of meadows, to the top of the hill.
To the left, the face of the ascent is pitted
By all homicides and every battle,
And the sounds of disaster string out on a curve.
Behind the ascent on the right, the orient line
   of progression.

And while this band in the distance
Is made of the whirling, leaping sounds
Of conch shells and human nights,

The flowery softness of the stars and all the sky
Flows over the side of the slope
Like a basket poured out in our face,
And turns the abyss beneath us a flowering blue.

DAWN

I have kissed the summer dawn.

Before the palaces, nothing moved. The water lay dead.
Battalions of shadows still kept the forest road.

I walked, waking warm and vital breath,
While stones watched, and wings rose soundlessly.

My first adventure, in a path already gleaming
With a clear pale light,
Was a flower who told me its name.

I laughed at the blond *Wasserfall*
That threw its hair across the pines:
On the silvered summit, I came upon the goddess.

Then, one by one, I lifted her veils.
In the long walk, waving my arms.

Across the meadow, where I betrayed her to the cock.
In the heart of town she fled among steeples and domes,
And I hunted her, scrambling like a beggar on marble
    wharves.

Above the road, near a thicket of laurel,
I caught her in her gathered veils,
And smelled the scent of her immense body.
Dawn and the child fell together at the bottom of
    the wood.

When I woke, it was noon.

FLOWERS

On a slope of gold,
In ropes of silk, gray gauze, green velvet and crystal
 disks
Blackening like bronze in the sun, . . .
I watch digitalis unfold
Against a screen of silver filigree, of eyes, of hair.

  Glittering on agate, a shower of gold,
Mahogany pillars supporting an emerald dome,
Bunched streamers of white satin,

        And rubies subtly stemmed
Surround the water-rose.
Like a blue-eyed god in his silhouette of snow,
To marble terraces the sea and sky
Invite a throng of roses, young and strong.

ORDINARY NOCTURNE

One breath tears operatic rents in these partitions,
Destroys the pivots of eroded roofs,
Dispels the limits of the hearth,
Makes casements disappear.

Along the vine I came,
Using a gargoyle as a footrest,
And into this carriage which shows its age
In convex windowpanes, in rounded panels,
In torturous upholstery.

Hearse of my lonely sleep,
Shepherd's cart of my stupidity . . .
The vehicle spins on the grass of an overgrown
    highway;
In a blemish high on the right window
Revolve pale lunar fictions, breasts and leaves.

A very dark green and a very dark blue blot out
    the image.
We unhitch and unharness beside a patch of gravel.

– Here we will whistle for storms, for Sodoms
    and Solymans,
For wild beasts and armies.

(Postilion and dream horses will ride on
        through more dense and suffocating groves,
        to sink me to my eyelids in the silken spring.)

– And drive ourselves off, whipped through splashing
    water
And spilled drinks, to roll on the barking of bulldogs ...

One breath dispels the limits of the hearth.

SEASCAPE

Silver and copper the cars –
    Steel and silver the prows –
Beating the foam, and
  Heaving up the briar-bush stumps.

The prairie tides,
    And the deep ruts in the ebbing sea
    Wind in circles away to the east –
To the pillars of forests,
  The pilings of wharves,
In an angle attacked by tornadoes of light!

WINTER FESTIVAL

Behind the comic-opera huts, the sound of a waterfall.

In the orchards and walks that border the stream,
Girandoles prolong the greens and reds of sunset.

Nymphs out of Horace in Empire coiffures . . .

    Siberian dances . . .

        Chinese ladies out of Boucher.

SCENES

The Old Comedy pursues its conventions and divides
   Its idylls:

      Boulevards of mountebanks' booths.
      A long wooden pier the length of a stony field
Where a savage crowd swirls beneath bare trees.

      Down corridors of black gauze, following the
          path
Of strollers under lanterns and leaves,

      Bird-actors come crashing down upon a stone
          pontoon
Propelled by the canopied archipelago of spectators'
   barges.

      Lyric scenes, to the sound of the flute and the
          drum,
Bow in spaces set apart on the ceilings
In modern clubrooms or in ancient Oriental halls.

This magic maneuvers high in an amphitheater
Crowned with bushes –
Or quivers and modulates for Boetians
In the shade of a moving wood, on the slopes of
    planted fields.

The operetta divides upon a stage

At the intersection of ten panels hung from the
    balcony
To the footlights.

BOTTOM

The thorns of reality being too sharp for my noble
    character –
I found myself nevertheless in my lady's bower,
    A great gray-blue bird, rising
    To the moldings of the ceiling
    Trailing a wing in the shadow of evening.
There I was the supporter to a baldachin
That upheld her favorite jewels,
And the exquisite work of her body . . .

A great bear with violet gums, sorrowfully
    whitening hair,
Crystal eyes shining like sideboard silver.

                The world became shadow . . .
                A glowing aquarium.
But in the morning – a battlesome morning in June –
I ran like an Ass,
Braying about the wood, brandishing my grievance,
Until the Sabines of the suburbs came,
Came leaping at my breast.

H

The mirror of the movements of Hortense
Images everything monstrous.
Her solitude is erotic mechanics,
Her lassitude the dynamics of love.
Under the guard of her childhood, she has been
For numerous ages and ages
The fiery purge of the race.
Her door is always open to suffering; there,
Human morality dissolves in her passion, or in
   her acts.

The terrible shudder of hesitant love
On bleeding ground, in a hydrogen glare!

                    Seek out Hortense.

155

DEMOCRACY

'Toward that intolerable country
    The banner floats along,
And the rattle of the drum is stifled
    By our rough backcountry shouting ...'

'In the metropolis we will feed
    The most cynical whoring.
We will destroy all logical revolt.'

'On to the languid scented lands!
    Let us implement industrial
And military exploitations.'

'Goodbye to all this, and never mind where.
    Conscripts of good intention,
We will have policies unnameable and animal.
    Knowing nothing of science, depraved in
        our pleasures,
To hell with the world around us rolling ...

    'This is the real advance!
                    Forward ...
                            March!'

HISTORIC EVENING

All in some night, let's say, where a simple tourist
   stands
Rescued from our economic nightmares,
The hand of a master wakes the pastoral harpsichord,
The face of the pond remembers queens and
   courtesans,
And beneath its glass the game of cards goes on –
Saints and sails, strung against the sunset,
Threads of harmony and half-forgotten iridescence.

     He trembles at the passing of hunts and hordes.

Dribblings of comedy on platforms of grass ...
The hesitations of paupers and cripples on these
   stupid stages!

Before his captive vision,
Germany schemes its way toward the heavens,
The deserts of Tartary lie, transformed with light,
The heart of the Celestial Empire crawls with
   ancient revolts;
On stairways and armchairs of rock, a pale flat world,
Africa and Occidents, will rise.

And a ballet of oceans and nights remembered,
Worthless chemistry, impossible melodies.

At every place the stagecoach stops,
The same bourgeois magic!

The youngest physicists understand
That we can no longer submit to an atmosphere
    so personal,
To this mist of physical remorse,
Whose very diagnosis is a sickness itself.

No! This is the time of the sweat bath, of oceans
    boiling over,
Of underground explosions, of the planet whirled
    away,
Of exterminations sure to follow;
Certainties only vaguely indicated in the Bible,
– Or by the Norns –
Which the serious man will be asked to observe.

Though the entire effect will be scarcely one of legend!

AFTER THE FLOOD

As soon as the thought of the Flood had subsided,
A rabbit stopped in the clover and trembling bell
    flowers,
And said his prayers to the rainbow, through a
    spider's web.

    Oh! what precious stones lay hidden,
    What flowers were already looking down.

In the dirty main street they hung up signs on
    their shops,
And dragged off boats to the sea, up there, fixed
    as if engraved.

In Bluebeard's Castle, the blood ran –
In slaughterhouses, in the circuses, where the
    seal of God
Paled at the windows. Blood flowed, and milk.

The beavers were building; coffee glasses steamed
    in the little cafés.

In the great house, its windowpanes still streaming,
Children in mourning looked at marvelous picture
    books.

A door slammed – and on the village square, a child
    waved his arms,
Making windmills and weathercocks everywhere,
Beneath a drizzling rain.

Madame X set up a piano in the Alps. Masses and
    first Communions
Were offered at the hundred thousand altars of the
    cathedral.

Caravans departed. The Hotel Splendide was erected
In a chaos of ice and polar night.

Since then, the Moon has heard the jackals,
Wailing in a desert full of thyme, and wooden-footed
    eclogues
Clumping in the orchard. Then, within a violet
    budding grove,
Eucharis told me it was spring.

Rise, pond – Foam, roll
Over the bridge and through the woods;
Black hangings and organ music, lightning and
    thunder –
Rise up in torrents;
Waters and sadness, rise and raise up the Floods!

For since they have swept on and vanished —

Oh burrowing jewels, oh open flowers . . .

What a bore!
And the Queen, the Witch who lights her fire
    in an earthen pot,
Will never tell us what she knows,
And we do not.

VAGABONDS

Pitiful brother! What terrible sleepless nights he
  caused me!

'I was never strongly in control of that undertaking.
I took advantage of his weakness.
Through my fault we would have gone back into exile,
Into slavery.'
He credited me with a strange ill luck, a strange
  innocence –
But for disturbing reasons.

I would answer this satanic doctor with sneers, and end
By leaving through the window. I was creating,
  beyond a country
Haunted with bands of rare music, the ghosts of future
  nocturnal debauch.

After this vaguely hygienic distraction, I would
  stretch out
On a pallet of straw. And almost every evening,
  no sooner asleep,
My poor brother would rise up, with stinking mouth
  and gouged eyes –
As he dreamt himself! – and drag me into the next
  room, howling
His dreams of idiot sorrow.

162

I had in all sincerity of mind undertaken to return him
To his primitive state of child of the Sun, and we used
    to wander,
Nourished on the wine of caverns and the dry bread
    of travelers,
While I searched continually to find the place and
    the formula.

LINES

When the world comes down to this one dark wood
Before our four astonished eyes ...
To a beach for two faithful children ...
To a house of music, for our clear accord ...
 I will find you.

Let there be no one here below but one old man,
Beautiful and calm, surrounded with 'unimagined
 luxury' ...
 I will be at your feet.

Let me penetrate all of your memories ...
Let me be *that woman* who can bind you hand and foot ...
 I will strangle you.

When we are very strong – who can hold us back?
And very gay – how can ridicule harm us?
When we are very bad – what can they do to us?
 Dress yourself up,
 And dance,
 And laugh.
I could never throw Love out the window.

My companion, my beggar girl, monstrous child!
How little you care,
About these unhappy women, about the intrigues
    of misfortune,
About my own extremity.

        Beguile us with your impossible voice –
            That voice!
The single flatterer of our abject despair.

A lowering morning in July.
A taste of ashes fills the air;
A smell of sweating wood stains the hearth.
                            Drowned flowers,
The spoils of long walks . . .
    A misty rain from canals beyond the fields.

Why not even trinkets and incense?

I have strung ropes from steeple to steeple;
Garlands from window to window;
And golden chains from star to star . . .

                        And I dance.

Smoke always rises from the distant pond.
What witch will ascend against the white sunset?
What violet streamers will come dropping down?

While the public funds dwindle in feasts of fraternity,
A bell of rosy fire rings in the clouds.

Breathing a sweet smell of India ink,
A powdery blackness drifts slowly over my lateness . . .
I lower the lights, lie down on my bed,
And, rolled into the shadows, I see you —

My darlings, my queens!

DEVOTION

To sister Louise Vanaen de Voringhem: her blue
   habit flapping
By the North Sea. For picking up castaways.

To sister Léonie Aubois d'Ashby: Boo! the grass
   of summer,
Buzzing and stinking. For fever in mothers and
   children.

To Lulu ... a demon ... who has kept a taste
   for churches
From the days of girlfriends and her incomplete
   education. For men.

To Madame X.

To the adolescent I was. To this holy old man,
   hermitage
Or mission.

To the spirit of the poor. And to high-ranking clergy.

As well to all worship, in any place of memorial
     worship
Among any events which it may be necessary
     to attend,
According to the aspirations of the moment,
Or even our own important vices.

This evening, to Circeto and her tall mirrors,
     fat as fish,
Painted like the ten months of red night
     (Her heart of amber and smoldering fuze)
For my lonely prayer silent as these regions of night,
Proceeding from exploits more violent than this
     polar chaos.

At any cost and in every air, even on metaphysical
     voyages.

     But that's all over.

TO A REASON

Your finger strikes the drum, dispersing all its sounds,
And new harmony begins.

Your step is the rise of new men, their setting out.

You turn away your head: New Love!
You turn your head again: New Love!

'Alter our fates, destroy our plagues,
Beginning with Time,' sing the children.
They beg of you: 'Make out of anything
The stuff of our fortunes and desires.'

Come from always, you will go away everywhere.

DRUNKEN MORNING

Oh, *my* Beautiful! Oh, *my* Good!
Hideous fanfare where yet I do not stumble!
    Oh, rack of enchantments!
For the first time, hurrah for the unheard-of work,
For the marvelous body! For the first time!

      It began with the laughter of children, and there
        it will end.

This poison will stay in our veins even when,
  as the fanfares depart,
We return to our former disharmony.
Oh, now, we who are so worthy of these tortures!
Let us re-create ourselves after that superhuman
  promise
Made to our souls and our bodies at their creation:
    That promise, that madness!
    Elegance, silence, violence!
They promised to bury in shadows the tree of
  good and evil,
To banish tyrannical honesty,
So that we might flourish in our very pure love.

It began with a certain disgust, and it ended –
Since we could not immediately seize upon
    eternity –
It ended in a scattering of perfumes.

Laughter of children, discretion of slaves, austerity
    of virgins,
Horror of faces and objects here below,
Be sacred in the memory of the evening past.

It began in utter boorishness, and now it ends
In angels of fire and ice.

Little drunken vigil, blessed!
If only for the mask that you have left us!
Method, we believe in you! We never forget that
    yesterday
You glorified all of our ages.
We have faith in poison.
We will give our lives completely, every day.

FOR THIS IS THE ASSASSINS' HOUR.

LIVES

I

Oh, the enormous avenues of the holy land . . .
    the terraces of the Temple!
What have they done with the Brahman who taught
    me the Proverbs?
From then, from far below, I can still see even those
    old women . . .
I remember hours of silver and sun near rivers,
With the hand of the countryside upon my shoulder,
And I remember our embraces, standing in the scented
    plain.

A flight of scarlet pigeons thunders about my thoughts . . .

In my exile here, I have a stage where I can play
The sweeping tragedies of all literatures.
I will show you unheard-of riches. I watch the history
Of the treasures you have found. I can see what will
    follow!
But my wisdom is as much ignored as chaos.
What is my nonbeing, compared with the stupor which
    awaits you?

II

I am an inventor much more deserving,
Different from all who have preceded me;
A musician, even, who has found something which may
be the key to love.
At present, gentleman of a bleak countryside beneath
a frugal sky,
I attempt to awaken my feelings in the memory of a
wandering childhood,
Of my apprenticeship, my arrival in wooden shoes . . .
of polemics,
Of five or six widowhoods, and of several wild nights
where my hard head
Kept me from reaching the exaltation of my
companions.
I do not regret my former share of divine gaiety;
The frugal air of this bleak countryside
Fortifies very effectively my atrocious skepticism.
But as this skepticism can no longer be put to work,
And since I am now devoted to a new preoccupation . . .
I expect to become a very wicked madman.

III

In an attic where I was locked up at the age of twelve,
I found out the world ... I made illustrations for the
Human Comedy.
In a closet I learned my history.
At an evening celebration in a northern town, I met
all the women
Of the painters of the past.
In an old alley in Paris, I was taught the classic
sciences.
In a magnificent house encircled by the Orient entire,
I brought my life's work to completion, and I passed
my illustrious retirement.
I have drunk my own blood. My task has been lifted
from me ...
No longer must I even think of it.
I am actually from beyond the grave ...

                                     and can do nothing for you.

DEPARTURE

Everything seen ...
    The vision gleams in every air.

Everything had ...
    The far sound of cities, in the evening,
    In sunlight, and always.

Everything known ...
    O Tumult! O Visions! These are the stops of life.

Departure in affection, and shining sounds.

ROYALTY

On a brilliant morning, in a city of *lovely* people,
A wonderful man and a wonderful woman
Were shouting out loud, in the middle of town:
  'Oh, my friends ... I want her to be queen!'
  '*I* want to be a queen!'
She kept on laughing and trembling,
While he talked to his friends about revelations,
And tribulations at an end.
They laughed and they leaned close to one another.
And, of course, they *were* royal ...
All morning long, when scarlet draperies hung upon
    all the houses,
And even in the afternoon,
When they appeared at the edge of the gardens
    of palms.

WORKERS

A warm morning in February.
The inopportune South came to revive our memories
Of being ridiculous paupers, of our young poverty.

Henrika had a cotton skirt with brown and white
    checks,
Probably worn in the century past,
A little hat with ribbons and a kerchief made of silk.
It looked sadder than mourning clothes.

We went for a walk in the suburbs.
The sky was heavy, and that wind from the South
Sharpened the sour smells that rose from trampled
    gardens,
And fields half dead.

This did not depress my wife so much as me.

In a puddle still standing from the previous month's
    flood,
On a rather high path, she pointed out some tiny
    little fish.

The city, with its smoke and the sounds of its trades
Crept behind us, far along the roads . . .
   Oh, other world, sky-blessed land of shade!
The South made me remember the terrible times of
   my childhood,
My summer despairs, the horrible amount of strength
   and knowledge
That fate always kept far from me.
   No! We will spend no summers in this grasping
     land,
   Where we will forever be nothing but orphans
     betrothed.

This hardened arm will drag along no more
   'sweet memories.'

BRIDGES

Crystal gray skies.

An odd pattern of bridges, some straight, some round,
Others cutting in or going off at angles on the others;
These images repeat themselves in the lighted curves
    of the canal,
But all so long and light that the banks, covered with
    domes,
Seem to lower and shrink.
Some of these bridges are still covered with masonry.
Others hold up masts, signals, fragile parapets.
Minor chords cross and disappear.
Ropes rise from the banks.
I can make out a red jacket, other costumes, and
    musical instruments.
Are these popular songs, bits of lordly concerts,
Remnants of public hymns?
The water is gray and blue, wide as an arm of the sea.

A white light falling from the heights of heaven
Obliterates this scene.

CITY

I am a temporary and not at all discontented citizen
Of a metropolis considered modern because all known
    taste has been eluded
In the furnishings and the outsides of the houses,
As well as in the plan of the city.
Here you will find no trace of a single monument
    to superstition.
Morals and language have been reduced
To their simplest expression, that is all!
These millions of people with no need to know
    each other
Lay down so equally the path of education, of trade
    and old age,
That the course of life is probably several times shorter
Than anything a crazy statistic sets up for people
    on the continent.
And from my window, what original specters roll
Through this thick eternal smoke—
Our Crowded Shade, our Midsummer Night!
Latter-day Erinys fly before this cottage
Which is my country and the depth of my heart,
Because everything here looks like this:
Dry-eyed Death, our diligent daughter and servant,
A hopeless Love and a pretty Crime wailing in the mud of
    the road.

WHEEL RUTS

On the right the summer morning stirs the leaves,
Waking mists and noises in this corner of the park ...
The slopes upon the left hide
In their violet shade
A thousand moving ruts in the damp road.

                    Parade of Enchantments.
This is how it was:
Chariots carrying animals of gilded wood,
Masts and motley tents,
Twenty spotted circus horses at a great gallop,
And children and men, on the most amazing beasts ...

Twenty studded carriages, with banners and
      with flowers,
Like faraway fairy tale coaches, full
Of little children, all dressed up
For a suburban pastorale ...

Even the coffins under their canopies
Flourish their ebony plumes,
And out trot great fat blue black mares.

PROMONTORY

The golden dawn and a shivering evening
Discover our boat lying along the coast
Below this villa and its outbuildings,
A promontory vast as Epirus and the Peloponnesus,
As the great isle of Japan,
As Arabia!
Shrines that glow with the return of processions;
Vast views of modern coastal fortifications;
Dunes patterned with burning flowers and
    bacchanales;
The great canals of Carthage and embankments
Of a sinister Venice; soft eruptions of Etnas,
Crevasses of flowers and melting glaciers;
Washhouses in a grove of German poplars;
The slopes of unusual gardens
Rise above Japanese trees;
The circular façades of the 'Royals' and 'Grands'
Of Scarborough or Brooklyn;
Their overhanging railways parallel and plumb
The appointments of this hotel,
Taken from the most elegant and colossal
    constructions
In the history of Italy, America, and Asia,
Whose windows and terraces, at present full of lights,
Of drinks and heady breezes,

Open in the minds of travelers and noblemen
Who permit, at every hour of the day,
Every tarantella of the seashore,
Every ritornello of the valleys of art,
To deck with miracles
The face of Promontory Palace.

CITIES I

This is what cities are like!

For this people they have raised these Alleghenies
and these Lebanons in dreams!
Chalets of wood, chalets of crystal
move along rails on invisible pulleys.
Ancient craters surrounded by colossi and by coppery
    palms
bellow melodious fires.
Gabbling parties of lovers echo on canals
strung out behind the chalets.
The rush of pealing bells cries out in gorges.

Corporations of giant singers assemble in robes
    and haloes
brighter than the white light of high peaks.
On platforms in passes, Rolands trumpet defiance.
On catwalks in the pit, from the roofs of country inns
The fires of heaven hang suspended from poles.
Crumbling apotheoses fall in high fields
where seraphic centaurs spin among avalanches.

Beyond the highest cliffs, upon a sea
that labors in the eternal birth of Venus,
swept in swarms by Orpheonic fleets, vibrant
with pearls and strange conches,
the shadow of a deathly brightness
sometimes dims the waves.

From hillsides breathes the soughing sound
of harvests of flowers as large as our weapons,
    our vessels.
In opaline procession, flashing
Mabs in russet wrappings wind
down into deep ravines.
In a waterfall
high in a towering hoof-trodden thorn thicket,
Diana gives suck to her stags.

Suburban Bacchantes wail; the moon growls
    and burns.
Venus visits the blacksmiths, the recluses,
in their caves.

The ideas of peoples sound from thickly clustering
    bell towers.
Unknown music vibrates in towering castles of bone.
All legend evolves, and excitement
rushes through the streets.
A paradise of whirlwinds melts away.
Savages dance, endlessly
dancing the Triumph of Night.
And once I went down into the tumult of Baghdad
in a boulevard, where companies shouted the joys of
    new labor
into thick air, restlessly moving
but never escaping those phantoms come down
from the heights where we were to have met.
What strong arms, what shining hour
will bring me back this country,
the source of my repose,
moving the least of my movements?

CITIES II

The official acropolis outdoes
The most colossal conceits of modern barbarity.
How can I describe the dull daylight of unchanging
    gray skies,
The imperial effect of these buildings, the eternally
    snow-covered ground?
Here, with an odd flair for enormity,
Are reconstructed all the wonders of classical
    architecture.
I visit expositions of paintings
In halls twenty times the size of Hampton Court.
What paintings!
A Norwegian Nebuchadnezzar commanded the
    staircases of the ministries;
The mere subalterns I caught sight of are prouder
    than Brahmans;
I trembled at the look of the guards before the colossi
And the building officials.
In the arrangement of buildings in squares, courts,
    and covered terraces,
They have done away with hacks and cabs.
The parks are examples of primitive nature
Ordered with marvelous art.

The upper town has strange sections;
An arm of the sea rolls empty, a blanket of blue
     hailstones,
Between quays covered with candelabra.
A short bridge leads to a postern gate
Directly under the dome of the Holy Chapel.
     This dome is an armature of wrought steel
     Fifteen thousand feet in approximate diameter.

At several points, from the copper causeways,
     the platforms,
The stairs that wind through the markets, that twist
     around the pillars,
I thought I could plumb the depth of the city!
This prodigy eternally amazes me:
How far above or below the acropolis is the rest
     of the city?
For the stranger in our time, recognition is impossible.
The commercial quarter is a circus in a single style,
With galleries in arcade. No shops are seen,
Yet the snow on the pavements is trampled;
Occasional nabobs, rare as Sunday-morning strollers
     in London,
Approach a diamond carriage. Occasional red velvet
     divans;
They serve cold drinks
At prices from eight hundred to eight thousand rupees.

I think of looking for theaters on this circus,
But I decide that the shops will contain dark dramas
    enough –
I believe there exists a police; but the law must be
    so different,
I cannot imagine what criminals here must be like.

The suburb, elegant as a Paris street,
Bathes in an air made of light –
The democratic element comprises some hundred
    souls.
Here again, the houses do not stretch out beyond
    each other;
The suburb disappears oddly into the country –
    the 'County' –
That fills the enduring west with forests
And prodigious plantations
Where savage noblemen hunt down their memoirs
Beneath a light we have created.

METROPOLITAN

From the indigo straits to the oceans of Ossian,
Across orange and rosy sands washed in the
    wine-dark sky
Boulevards of crystal rise, crisscross –

They swarm instantly with the young families of
    the poor,
Fed from the fruit-sellers' stands – Nothing too rich.

                        This is the city!

Fleeing out of the bituminous waste
In rout through sheets of mist rising in terrible bands
To the hovering sky, high, then low, full of the
    blackest,
Most sinister smoke of a mourning Ocean,
        Roll helmets, wheels, wagons, and horses' flanks –

                        This is battle!

Lift up your head: this high-arched wooden bridge,
The straggling kitchen gardens of Samaria;
Painted masks beneath a lantern beaten by cold nights,
A stupid water nymph in shrieking garments
Deep in the riverbed.
Gleaming skulls in the garden vines,

And other phantasmagorias –

                    This is the country.

Highways edged with iron grilles and walls,
Barely holding back their groves,
The terrible flowers called sisters, called hearts –
Damascus damned and endless –
The holdings of enchanted aristocracies
(High Rhenish, Japanese, Guaranian)
Still fit to resound with the music of the ancients,
– There are inns that will never ever open again;
There are princesses, and (if you are not yet
   overwhelmed)
The stars to gaze at –

                    This is the sky.

The morning when, with Her, you struggled
In the glaring snow; green lips, ice, black banners,
Blue rays of light,
And the dark red perfumes of the polar sun –

This is your strength.

ANGUISH

Can she make me forgive my constantly defeated
    ambitions –
Can an easy finale repair ages of misery –
Can a day of success destroy the shame
Of our fatal lack of skill?

    (O palms! Diamond! Love! Strength!
    Beyond all joys and glories!
    Everywhere, in every way, demon and god!
    The Youth of this being: Myself!)

Can accidents of scientific magic and movements
Of fraternal union be considered a slow return
To time remembered before our fall from grace?

But the Vampire who makes us kind
Expects us to be entertained with what she leaves us,
Or in another way to be much more amusing.

Convulsed with wounds from the dying air and the sea,
Racked by the murderous silence of water and air,
By torments that laugh, their silence a terrible howl.

BARBARIAN

Long after days and seasons pass,
And the living have gone, and the land,

A Banner of meat that bleeds
Onto the silk of seas and arctic flowers;
(they do not exist).

Echoes of heroics, and the old fanfares
That still attack us, head and heart –
Far from the assassins of the past,

A Banner of meat that bleeds
Onto the silk of seas and arctic flowers;
(they do not exist).

Delight!
   Bright fires, raining in squalls of sleet –
Delight!
   Fires in the rain of a diamond wind
Thrown from this terrestrial core, charred forever,
And for us.
O World!
   (Far from old retreats and ancient flames we hear
      and feel.)
Bright fires and foam. Music, turning in crevices;
The shock of ice against the stars.

O Delight, O music, O world!

   There . . .
Forms; sweating, hair and eyes, drifting . . .
White tears, burning tears . . . O delight!
The voice of Woman in gulfs of fire,
and frozen caves of ice.

   And a Banner . . .

WAR

When I was a child,
my vision was refined in certain skies;
my face is the product of every nuance.
All Phenomena were aroused.
At present, the eternal inflections of the moment
and the infinity of mathematics hunt me over this earth
where I experience all civil successes,
respected by strange childhood and devouring
affections.

I envisage a war, of justice or strength,
of a logic beyond all imagining.
It is as simple as a musical phrase.

MOVEMENT

A winding movement on the slope beside the rapids
    of the river.
The abyss at the stern,
The swiftness of the incline,
The overwhelming passage of the tide,
With extraordinary lights and chemical wonders
Lead on the travelers
Through the windspouts of the valley
And the whirlpool.

These are the conquerors of the world,
Seeking their personal chemical fortune;
Sport and comfort accompany them;
They bring education for races, for classes, for animals
Within this vessel, rest and vertigo
In diluvian light,
In terrible evenings of study.

For in this conversation in the midst of machines,
Of blood, of flowers, of fire, of jewels,
In busy calculations on this fugitive deck,
Is their stock of studies visible
   – Rolling like a dike beyond
   The hydraulic propulsive road,
   Monstrous, endlessly lighting its way –
Themselves driven into harmonic ecstasy
And the heroism of discovery.

Amid the most amazing accidents,
Two youths stand out alone upon the ark
   – Can one excuse past savagery? –
And sing, upon their watch.

SALE

For sale –
 Whatever the Jews have left unsold,
What nobleness and crime have never tasted,
What damned love cannot know,
What is strange to the infernal probity of the masses,
What time and science need not recognize:

 Voices reconstituted;
A fraternal awakening of all choral and orchestral
  energies
and their immediate application.
The occasion, the unique moment, to set our senses
  free!

For sale –
 Priceless Bodies, beyond race or world or sex or
   line of descent!
Riches in ubiquitous flood!
Unrestricted sales of diamonds!

For sale –
 Anarchy for the masses;
Wild satisfaction for knowing amateurs;
Atrocious death for the faithful and for lovers!

For sale –

Homesteads and migrations, sports,
Enchantment and perfect comfort, and the noise,
the movement, and the future they entail.

For sale –

Extravagant uses of calculation, unknown
harmonic intervals.
Discoveries and unsuspected terms, immediately
available.

Senseless and infinite flight toward invisible
splendor,
Toward insensible delight –
The madness of its secrets shocks all known vice!
The mob is aghast at its gaiety!

For sale –

Bodies and voices, immense and unquestionable
opulence,
Stuff that will never be sold.

The sellers sell on!
Salesmen may turn in their accounts later …

GENIE

He is love and the present because he has opened
    our house
to winter's foam and to the sounds of summer,
He who purified all that we drink and eat;
He is the charm of passing places,
the incarnate delight of all things that abide.
He is affection and the future, the strength and love
that we, standing surrounded by anger and weariness,
See passing in the storm-filled sky
and in banners of ecstasy.

He is love, perfect and rediscovered measure,
Reason, marvelous and unforeseen,
Eternity: beloved prime mover of the elements,
    of destinies.
We all know the terror of his yielding, and of ours:
Oh, delight of our well-being, brilliance
of our faculties, selfish affection and passion
for him, who loves us forever ...

And we remember him, and he goes on his way...
And if Adoration departs, then it sounds, his promise
    sounds:
    'Away with these ages and superstitions,
    These couplings, these bodies of old!
    All our age has submerged.'

He will not go away, will not come down again from
    some heaven.
He will not fulfill the redemption of women's fury
nor the gaiety of men nor the rest of this sin:
For he is and he is loved, and so it is already done.

Oh, his breathing, the turn of his head when he runs:
Terrible speed of perfection in action and form!
Fecundity of spirit and vastness of the universe!

    His body! Release so long desired,
The splintering of grace before a new violence!

    Oh, the sight, the sight of him!
All ancient genuflections, all sorrows are *lifted* as he
    passes.

    The light of his day!
All moving and sonorous suffering dissolves in more
    intense music.

In his step there are vaster migrations
than the old invasions were.
    Oh, He and we! a pride more benevolent than
        charities lost.

    Oh, world! and the shining song of new sorrows.

He has known us all and has loved us.
Let us discover how, this winter night, to hail him
    from cape to cape, from the unquiet pole to the
        château,
    from crowded cities to the empty coast,
    from glance to glance, with our strength and our
        feelings exhausted,
To see him, and to send him once again away . . .
And beneath the tides and over high deserts of snow
To follow his image,
his breathing, his body, the light of his day.

YOUTH

All calculations set to one side;
The inevitable Descent from Heaven,
A visitation of memories and a seance of rhythms
Invades the house, my head,
    And the world of the mind.

A horse leaps forward on suburban turf,
Past planted fields and stretches of woods
Misty with carbonic plague.
A wretched theatrical woman, somewhere in the
    world,
Sighs after an improbable indulgence.
Desperadoes lie dreaming of storm, and of wounds
    and debauch.
Along small streams the little children sit,
    Stifling their curses.

Let us turn once more to our studies,
To the noise of insatiable movement
That forms and ferments in the masses.

II. SONNET

Man of average constitution, was the flesh not once
A fruit, hanging in an orchard?

                        O infant hours!

Was the body not a treasure to be unsparing of?
Oh, Loving – either Psyche's peril, or her strength.
    In princes and artists, the earth had fertile
        watersheds,
But the suite of generations and race
Drives us to crime and to mourning –
The world is our salvation and our danger.
At present, with this labor completed,
You – your calculations,
You – your impatience,
Are reduced to no more than your dancing, your voice,
Indeterminate, unforced,
Yet reason for a double occasion of invention and
    success;
Quiet fraternal humanity in an imageless universe.
Strength and justice shine through this dancing,
    this voice,
    That only the present can appreciate.

III. TWENTY YEARS OLD

Exiled the voices of instruction;
Physical ingenuousness staled in bitterness ...
                      ... Adagio.

Ah! The endless egoism of adolescence,
Its studious optimism:
    How the world this summer was full of flowers!
Dying airs, dying shapes ...
A chorus to appease impotence and absence!
A chorus of glasses of nocturnal melodies ...

(Of course, our nerves are quickly shot to hell!)

IV

You are playing still at the temptation of Saint Anthony –
The looseness of failing zeal, tics of puerile pride,
Faltering and fright.
But you will undertake this task;
All the possibilities of Harmony and Architecture
Rise up about your seat. Unlooked for,
Creatures of perfection will throng your experience.
Dreaming around you will hover the curiosity
Of forgotten crowds and halting luxuries.
Your memories and your senses will become
The food of your creative impulses.

And what of the world?
What will it become when you leave it?
    Nothing, nothing at all like its present appearance.

PROSE

A SEASON IN HELL

'ONCE, IF MY MEMORY SERVES ME WELL'

Once, if my memory serves me well, my life was a banquet where every heart revealed itself, where every wine flowed.

One evening I took Beauty in my arms – and I thought her bitter – and I insulted her.

I steeled myself against justice.

I fled. O witches, O misery, O hate, my treasure was left in your care ...

I have withered within me all human hope. With the silent leap of a sullen beast, I have downed and strangled every joy.

I have called for executioners; I want to perish chewing on their gun butts. I have called for plagues, to suffocate in sand and blood. Unhappiness has been my god. I have lain down in the mud, and dried myself off in the crime-infested air. I have played the fool to the point of madness.

And springtime brought me the frightful laugh of an idiot.

Now recently, when I found myself ready to *croak!* I thought to seek the key to the banquet of old, where I might find an appetite again.

That key is Charity. (This idea proves I was dreaming!)

'You will stay a hyena, etc....,' shouts the demon who once crowned me with such pretty poppies. 'Seek death with all your desires, and all selfishness, and all the Seven Deadly Sins.'

Ah, I've taken too much of that: still, dear Satan, don't look so annoyed, I beg you! And while waiting for a few belated cowardices, since you value in a writer all lack of descriptive or didactic flair, I pass you these few foul pages from the diary of a Damned Soul.

BAD BLOOD

From my ancestors the Gauls I have pale blue eyes, a narrow brain, and awkwardness in competition. I think my clothes are as barbaric as theirs. But I don't butter my hair.

The Gauls were the most stupid hide-flayers and hay-burners of their time.

From them I inherit: idolatry, and love of sacrilege – oh, all sorts of vice; anger, lechery – terrific stuff, lechery – lying, above all, and laziness.

I have a horror of all trades and crafts. Bosses and workers, all of them peasants, and common. The hand that holds the pen is as good as the one that holds the plow. (What a century for hands!) I'll never learn to use my hands. And then, domesticity goes too far. The propriety of beggary shames me. Criminals are as disgusting as men without balls; I'm intact, and I don't care.

But who has made my tongue so treacherous, that until now it has counseled and kept me in idleness? I have not used even my body to get along. Out-idling the sleepy toad, I have lived everywhere. There's not one family in Europe that I don't know. Families, I mean, like mine, who owe their existence to the Declaration of the Rights of Man. I have known each family's eldest son!

If only I had a link to some point in the history of France!

But instead, nothing.

I am well aware that I have always been of an inferior race. I cannot understand revolt. My race has never risen, except to plunder: to devour like wolves a beast they did not kill.

I remember the history of France, the Eldest Daughter of the Church. I would have gone, a village serf, crusading to the Holy Land; my head is full of roads in the Swabian plains, of the sight of Byzantium, of the ramparts of Jerusalem; the cult of Mary, the pitiful thought of Christ crucified, turns in my head with a thousand profane enchantments – I sit like a

213

leper among broken pots and nettles, at the foot of a wall eaten away by the sun. – And later, a wandering mercenary, I would have bivouacked under German nighttimes.

Ah! one thing more: I dance the Sabbath in a scarlet clearing, with old women and children.

I don't remember much beyond this land, and Christianity. I will see myself forever in its past. But always alone, without a family; what language, in fact, did I used to speak? I never see myself in the councils of Christ; nor in the councils of the Lords, Christ's representatives. What was I in the century past? I only find myself today. The vagabonds, the hazy wars are gone. The inferior race has swept over all – the People (as they put it), Reason; Nation and Science.

Ah, Science! Everything is taken from the past. For the body and the soul – the last sacrament – we have Medicine and Philosophy, household remedies and folk songs rearranged. And royal entertainments, and games that kings forbid. Geography, Cosmography, Mechanics, Chemistry!...

Science, the new nobility! Progress! The world moves!... And why shouldn't it?

We have visions of numbers. We are moving toward the *Spirit*. What I say is oracular and absolutely right. I understand ... and since I cannot express myself except in pagan terms, I would rather keep quiet.

Pagan blood returns! The Spirit is at hand ... why does Christ not help me, and grant my soul nobility and freedom? Ah, but the Gospel belongs to the past! The Gospel. The Gospel ...

I wait gluttonously for God. I have been of inferior race for ever and ever.

And now I am on the beaches of Brittany. ... Let cities light their lamps in the evening; my daytime is done, I am leaving Europe. The air of the sea will burn my lungs; lost climates will turn my skin to leather. To swim, to pulverize grass, to hunt, above all to smoke; to drink strong drinks, as strong as molten ore, as did those dear ancestors around their fires.

I will come back with limbs of iron, with dark skin, and angry eyes: in this mask, they will think I belong to a strong race. I will have gold; I will be brutal and indolent. Women nurse these ferocious invalids come back from the tropics. I will become involved in politics. Saved.

Now I am accursed, I detest my native land. The best thing is a drunken sleep, stretched out on some strip of shore.

But no one leaves. Let us set out once more on our native roads, burdened with my vice — that vice that since the age of reason has driven roots of suffering into my side — that towers to heaven, beats me, hurls me down, drags me on.

Ultimate innocence, final timidity. All's said. Carry no more my loathing and treacheries before the world.

Come on! Marching, burdens, the desert, boredom and anger.

Hire myself to whom? What beast adore? What sacred images destroy? What hearts shall I break? What lie maintain? Through what blood wade?

Better to keep away from justice. A hard life, outright stupor – with a dried-out fist to lift the coffin lid, lie down, and suffocate. No old age this way – no danger: terror is very un-French.

– Ah! I am so forsaken I will offer at any shrine impulses toward perfection.

Oh, my self-denial, my marvelous Charity, my Selfless Love! And still here below!

De profundis, Domine ... what an ass I am!

When I was still a little child, I admired the hardened convict on whom the prison door will always close; I used to visit the bars and the rented rooms his presence had consecrated; I saw *with his eyes* the blue sky and the flower-filled work of the fields; I followed his fatal scent through city streets. He had more strength than the saints, more sense than any explorer – and he, he alone! was witness to his glory and his rightness.

Along the open road on winter nights, homeless, cold, and hungry, one voice gripped my frozen heart:

'Weakness or strength: you exist, that is strength. ...
You don't know where you are going or why you are
going; go in everywhere, answer everyone. No one will
kill you, any more than if you were a corpse.' In the
morning my eyes were so vacant and my face so dead
that the people I met *may not even have seen me.*

In cities, mud went suddenly red and black, like a
mirror when a lamp in the next room moves, like
treasure in the forest! Good luck, I cried, and I saw a sea
of flames and smoke rise to heaven, and left and right all
wealth exploded like a billion thunderbolts.

But orgies and the companionship of women were
impossible for me. Not even a friend. I saw myself
before an angry mob, facing a firing squad, weeping out
sorrows they could not understand, and pardoning –
like Joan of Arc! – 'Priests, professors and doctors, you
are mistaken in delivering me into the hands of the law.
I have never been one of you; I have never been a
Christian; I belong to the race that sang on the scaffold;
I do not understand your laws; I have no moral sense; I
am a brute: you are making a mistake. . . .'

Yes, my eyes are closed to your light. I am an animal,
a nigger. But I can be saved. You are fake niggers;
maniacs, savages, misers, all of you. Businessman,
you're a nigger; judge, you're a nigger; general, you're a
nigger; emperor, old scratch-head, you're a nigger:
you've drunk a liquor no one taxes, from Satan's still.

217

This nation is inspired by fever and cancer. Invalids and old men are so respectable that they ask to be boiled. The best thing is to quit this continent where madness prowls, out to supply hostages for these wretches. I will enter the true kingdom of the sons of Ham.

Do I understand nature? Do I understand myself? *No more words.* I shroud dead men in my stomach. ... Shouts, drums, dance, dance, dance! I can't even imagine the hour when the white men land, and I will fall into nothingness.

Thirst and hunger, shouts, dance, dance, dance, dance!

The white men are landing! Cannons! Now we must be baptized, get dressed, and go to work.

My heart has been stabbed by grace. Ah! I hadn't thought this would happen.

But I haven't done anything wrong. My days will be easy, and I will be spared repentance. I will not have had the torments of the soul half-dead to the Good, where austere light rises again like funeral candles. The fate of a first-born son, a premature coffin covered with shining tears. No doubt, perversion is stupid, vice is stupid; rottenness must always be cast away. But the clock must learn to strike more than hours of pure pain! Am I to be carried away like a child, to play in paradise, forgetting all this misery?

Quick! Are there any other lives? Sleep for the rich is

impossible. Wealth has always lived openly. Divine love alone confers the keys of knowledge. I see that nature is only a show of kindness. Farewell chimeras, ideals and errors.

The reasonable song of angels rises from the rescue ship: it is divine love. Two loves! I may die of earthly love, die of devotion. I have left behind creatures whose grief will grow at my going. You choose me from among the castaways; aren't those who remain my friends?

Save them!

I am reborn in reason. The world is good. I will bless life. I will love my brothers. There are no longer childhood promises. Nor the hope of escaping old age and death. God is my strength, and I praise God.

Boredom is no longer my love. Rage, perversion, madness, whose every impulse and disaster I know – my burden is set down entire. Let us appraise with clear heads the extent of my innocence. I am no longer able to ask for the consolation of a beating. I don't imagine I'm off on a honeymoon with Jesus Christ for a father-in-law.

I am no prisoner of my own reason. I have said: God. I want freedom, within salvation: how shall I go about it? A taste for frivolity has left me. No further need for divine love or for devotion to duty. I do not regret the age of emotion and feeling. To each his own reason, contempt, Charity: I keep my place at the top of the angelic ladder of good sense.

As for settled happiness, domestic or not ... no, I can't. I am too dissipated, too weak. Work makes life blossom, an old idea, not mine; my life doesn't weigh enough, it drifts off and floats far beyond action, that third pole of the world.

What an old maid I'm turning into, to lack the courage to love death!

If only God would grant me that celestial calm, ethereal calm, and prayer – like the saints of old. – The Saints! They were strong! Anchorites, artists of a kind we no longer need....

Does this farce have no end? My innocence is enough to make me cry. Life is the farce we all must play.

Stop it! This is your punishment.... *Forward march!*

Ah! my lungs burn, my temples roar! Night rolls in my eyes, beneath this sun! My heart ... my arms and legs....

Where are we going? To battle? I am weak! the others go on ahead ... tools, weapons ... give me time!

Fire! Fire at me! Here! or I'll give myself up! – Cowards! – I'll kill myself! I'll throw myself beneath the horses' hooves!

Ah!...

– I'll get used to it.

That would be the French way, the path of honor!

NIGHT IN HELL

I have just swallowed a terrific mouthful of poison. –
Blessed, blessed, blessed the advice I was given!

– My guts are on fire. The power of the poison twists
my arms and legs, cripples me, drives me to the ground.
I die of thirst, I suffocate, I cannot cry. This is Hell,
eternal torment! See how the flames rise! I burn as I
ought to. Go on, Devil!

I once came close to a conversion to the good and to
felicity, salvation. How can I describe my vision; the air
of Hell is too thick for hymns! There were millions of
delightful creatures in smooth spiritual harmony,
strength and peace, noble ambitions, I don't know
what all.

Noble ambitions!

But I am still alive! Suppose damnation is eternal! A
man who wants to mutilate himself is certainly damned,
isn't he? I believe I am in Hell, therefore I am. This is
the catechism at work. I am the slave of my baptism.
You, my parents, have ruined my life, and your own.
Poor child! – Hell is powerless against pagans. – I am
still alive! Later on, the delights of damnation will
become more profound. A crime, quick, and let me fall to
nothingness, condemned by human law.

Shut up, will you shut up! Everything here is shame
and reproach – Satan saying that the fire is worthless,

that my anger is ridiculous and silly. – Ah, stop! ... those mistakes someone whispered – magic spells, deceptive odors, childish music – and to think that I possess the truth, that I can have a vision of justice: my judgment is sound and firm, I am prime for perfection. ... Pride. – My scalp begins to tighten. Have mercy! Lord, I'm afraid! Water, I thirst, I thirst! Ah, childhood, grass and rain, the puddle on the paving stones, *Moonlight, when the clock strikes twelve.* ... The devil is in the clock tower, right now! Mary! Holy Virgin! ... – Horrible stupidity.

Look there, are those not honorable men, who wish me well? Come on ... a pillow over my mouth, they cannot hear me, they are only ghosts. Anyway, no one ever thinks of anyone else. Don't let them come closer. I must surely stink of burning flesh. ...

My hallucinations are endless. This is what I've always gone through: the end of my faith in history, the neglect of my principles. I shall say no more about this; poets and visionaries would be jealous. I am the richest one of all, a thousand times, and I will hoard it like the sea.

O God – the clock of life stopped but a moment ago. I am no longer within the world. – Theology is accurate; hell is certainly *down below* – and heaven is up on high. Ecstasy, nightmare, sleep, in a nest of flames.

How the mind wanders idly in the country ... Satan,

Ferdinand, blows with the wild seed ... Jesus walks on purple thorns but doesn't bend them ... Jesus used to walk on troubled waters. In the light of the lantern we saw him there, all white, with long brown hair, standing in the curve of an emerald wave....

I will tear the veils from every mystery – mysteries of religion or of nature, death, birth, the future, the past, cosmogony, and nothingness. I am a master of phantasmagoria.

Listen!

Every talent is mine! – There is no one here, and there is someone: I wouldn't want to waste my treasure. – Shall I give you Afric chants, belly dancers? Shall I disappear, shall I begin an attempt to discover the *Ring?* Shall I? I will manufacture gold, and medicines.

Put your faith in me, then; faith comforts, it guides and heals. Come unto me all of you – even the little children – let me console you, let me pour out my heart for you – my miraculous heart! – Poor men, poor laborers! I do not ask for prayers; give me only your trust, and I will be happy.

Think of me, now. All this doesn't make me miss the world much. I'm lucky not to suffer more. My life was nothing but sweet stupidities, unfortunately.

Bah! I'll make all the ugly faces I can! We are out of the world, that's sure. Not a single sound. My sense of touch is gone. Ah, my château, my Saxony, my willow

woods! Evenings and mornings, nights and days. ...
How tired I am!

I ought to have a special hell for my anger, a hell for
my pride — and a hell for sex; a whole symphony of
hells!

I am weary, I die. This is the grave and I'm turning
into worms, horror of horrors! Satan, you clown, you
want to dissolve me with your charms. Well, I want it. I
want it! Stab me with a pitchfork, sprinkle me with fire!

Ah! To return to life! To stare at our deformities.
And this poison, this eternally accursèd embrace! My
weakness, and the world's cruelty! My God, have pity,
hide me, I can't control myself at all! I am hidden, and
I am not.

And as the Damned soul rises, so does the fire.

FIRST DELIRIUM: THE FOOLISH VIRGIN
THE INFERNAL BRIDEGROOM

Let us hear the confession of an old friend in Hell:

'O Lord, O Celestial Bridegroom, do not turn thy face from the confession of the most pitiful of thy handmaidens. I am lost. I'm drunk. I'm impure. What a life!

'Pardon, Lord in Heaven, pardon! Ah, pardon! All these tears! And all the tears to come later on, I hope!

'Later on, I will meet the Celestial Bridegroom! I was born to be *His* slave. – That other one can beat me now!

'Right now, it's the end of the world! Oh, girls ... my friends ... no, not my friends ... I've never gone through *anything* like this; delirium, torments, anything.... It's so silly!

'Oh, I cry, I'm suffering! I really am suffering! And still I've got a right to do whatever I want, now that I am covered with contempt by the most contemptible hearts.

'Well, let me make my confession anyway, though I may have to repeat it twenty times again – *so* dull, and *so* insignificant!

'I am a slave of the Infernal Bridegroom; the one who seduced the foolish virgins. That's exactly the devil he is. He's no phantom, he's no ghost. But I, who have lost my wits, damned and dead to the world – no one will be able to kill me – how can I describe him to you? I can't

225

even talk anymore! I'm all dressed in mourning, I'm crying, I'm afraid. Please, dear Lord, a little fresh air, if you don't mind, please!

'I am a widow – I used to be a widow – oh, yes, I used to be very serious in those days; I wasn't born to become a skeleton! He was a child – or almost. ... His delicate, mysterious ways enchanted me. I forgot all my duties in order to follow him. What a life we lead! True life is lacking. We are exiles from this world, really – I go where he goes; I *have* to. And lots of times he gets mad at me – at *me*, poor sinner! That Devil! (He really *is* a Devil, you know, and *not a man.*)

'He says: "I don't love women. Love has to be reinvented, we know that. The only thing women can ultimately imagine is security. Once they get that, love, beauty, everything else goes out the window. All they have left is cold disdain; that's what marriages live on nowadays. Sometimes I see women who ought to be happy, with whom I could have found companionship, already swallowed up by brutes with as much feeling as an old log. ..."

'I listen to him turn infamy into glory, cruelty into charm. "I belong to an ancient race: my ancestors were Norsemen: they slashed their own bodies, drank their own blood. I'll slash my body all over, I'll tattoo myself, I want to be as ugly as a Mongol; you'll see, I'll scream in the streets. I want to go really mad with anger. Don't show me jewels; I'll get down on all fours and writhe on the carpet. I want my wealth stained all over with blood. I will *never* do any work. ...." Several times, at night, his demon seized me, and we rolled about wrestling! – Sometimes at night when he's drunk he hangs around street corners or behind doors, to scare me to death. "I'll get my throat cut for sure, won't *that* be disgusting." And, oh, those days when he wants to go around pretending he's a criminal!

'Sometimes he talks, in his backcountry words, full of emotion, about death, and how it makes us repent, and how surely there are miserable people in the world, about exhausting work, and about saying goodbye and how it tears your heart. In the dives where we used to get drunk, he would cry when he looked at the people around us – cattle of the slums. He used to pick up drunks in the dark streets. He had the pity of a brutal mother for little children. He went around with all the sweetness of a little girl on her way to Sunday school. He pretended to know all about everything – business, art, medicine – and I always went along with him; I had to!

'I used to see clearly all the trappings that he hung up in his imagination; costumes, fabrics, furniture. ... It was I who lent him weapons, and a change of face. I could visualize everything that affected him, exactly as he would have imagined it for himself. Whenever he seemed depressed, I would follow him into strange, complicated adventures, on and on, into good and evil; but I always knew I could never be a part of his world. Beside his dear body, as he slept, I lay awake hour after hour, night after night, trying to imagine why he wanted so much to escape from reality. No man before had ever had such a desire. I was aware – without being afraid for him – that he could become a serious menace to society. Did he, perhaps, have secrets that would *remake life?* No, I told myself, he was only looking for them. but of course, his charity is under a spell, and I am its prisoner. No one else could have the strength – the strength of despair! – to stand it, to stand being cared for and loved by him. Besides, I could never imagine him with anybody else – we all have eyes for our own Dark Angel, never other people's Angels – at least I think so. I lived in his soul as if it were a palace that had been cleared out so that the most unworthy person in it would be you, that's all. Ah, *really*, I used to depend on him terribly. But what did he want with my dull, my cowardly existence? He couldn't improve me, though he never managed to kill me! I get so sad and disappointed; sometimes I say to him "I understand you." He just shrugs his shoulders.

'And so my heartaches kept growing and growing, and I saw myself going more and more to pieces (and everyone else would have seen it, too, if I hadn't been so miserable that no one even looked at me anymore!), and still more and more I craved his affection. . . . His kisses and his friendly arms around me were just like heaven – a dark heaven, that I could go into, and where I wanted only to be left – poor, deaf, dumb, and blind. Already, I was getting to depend on it. I used to imagine that we were two happy children free to wander in a Paradise of sadness. We were in absolute harmony. Deeply moved, we labored side by side. But then, after a piercing embrace, he would say: "How funny it will all seem, all you've gone through, when I'm not here anymore. When you no longer feel my arms around your shoulders, nor my heart beneath you, nor this mouth on your eyes. Because I will have to go away some day, far away. Besides, I've got to help out others too; that's what I'm here for. Although I won't really like it . . . dear heart. . . ." And in that instant I could feel myself, with him gone, dizzy with fear, sinking down into the most horrible blackness – into death. I made him promise that he would never leave me. And he promised, twenty times; promised like a lover. It was as meaningless as my saying to him: "I understand you."

'Oh, I've never been jealous of him. He'll never leave me, I'm sure of it. What will he do? He doesn't know a soul; he'll never work; he wants to live like a sleepwalker. Can his kindness and his charity by themselves give him his place in the real world? There are moments when I forget the wretched mess I've fallen into. ... He will give me strength; we'll travel, we'll go hunting in the desert, we'll sleep on the sidewalks of unknown cities, carefree and happy. Or else some day I'll wake up and his magic power will have changed all laws and morals, but the world will still be the same and leave me my desires and my joys and my lack of concern. Oh, that wonderful world of adventures that we found in children's books – won't you give me that world? I've suffered so much; I deserve a reward. ... He can't. I don't know what he *really* wants. He says he has hopes and regrets: but they have nothing to do with me. Does he talk to God? Maybe I should talk to God myself. I am in the depths of the abyss, and I have forgotten how to pray.

'Suppose he did explain his sadness to me – would I understand it any better than his jokes and insults? He attacks me, he spends hours making me ashamed of everything in the world that has ever meant anything to me, and then he gets mad if I cry.

'... "Do you see that lovely young man going into that beautiful, peaceful house? His name is Duval, Dufour; ... Armand, Maurice, whatever you please. There is a woman who has spent her life loving that evil creature; she died. I'm sure she's a saint in heaven right now. You are going to kill me the way he killed that woman. That's what's in store for all of us who have

unselfish hearts. ...." Oh, dear! There were days when
all men of action seemed to him like the toys of some
grotesque raving. He would laugh, horribly, on and on.
Then he would go back to acting like a young mother,
or an older sister. ... If he were not such a wild thing, we
would be saved! But even his sweetness is mortal. ... I
am his slave. ...

   'Oh, I've lost my mind!

   'Some day maybe he'll just disappear miraculously,
but I absolutely must be told about it, I mean if he's
going to go back up into heaven or someplace, so that I
can go and watch for just a minute the Assumption of
my darling boy. ...'

   One hell of a household!

SECOND DELIRIUM: THE ALCHEMY OF THE WORD

My turn now. The story of one of my insanities.

For a long time I boasted that I was master of all possible landscapes – and I thought the great figures of modern painting and poetry were laughable.

What I liked were: absurd paintings, pictures over doorways, stage sets, carnival backdrops, billboards, bright-colored prints, old-fashioned literature, church Latin, erotic books full of misspellings, the kind of novels our grandmothers read, fairy tales, little children's books, old operas, silly old songs, the naïve rhythms of country rimes.

I dreamed of Crusades, voyages of discovery that nobody had heard of, republics without histories, religious wars stamped out, revolutions in morals, movements of races and of continents; I used to believe in every kind of magic.

I invented colors for the vowels! A black, E white, I red, O blue, U green. I made rules for the form and movement of every consonant, and I boasted of inventing, with rhythms from within me, a kind of poetry that all the senses, sooner or later, would recognize. And I alone would be its translator.

I began it as an investigation. I turned silences and nights into words. What was unutterable, I wrote down. I made the whirling world stand still.

Far from flocks, from birds and country girls,
What did I drink within that leafy screen
Surrounded by tender hazelnut trees
In the warm green mist of afternoon?

What could I drink from this young Oise
– Tongueless trees, flowerless grass, dark skies –
Drink from these yellow gourds, far from the hut
I loved? Some golden draught that made me sweat.

I would have made a doubtful sign for an inn.
Later, toward evening, the sky filled with clouds ...
Water from the woods runs out on virgin sands,
And heavenly winds cast ice thick on the ponds;

Then I saw gold, and wept, but could not drink.

*

At four in the morning, in summertime,
Love's drowsiness still lasts ...
The bushes blow away the odor
Of the night's feast.

Beyond the bright Hesperides,
Within the western workshop of the Sun,
Carpenters scramble – in shirtsleeves –
    Work is begun.

And in desolate, moss-grown isles
They raise their precious panels
    Where the city
    Will paint a hollow sky.

For these charming dabblers in the arts
Who labor for a King in Babylon,
Venus! Leave for a moment
    Lovers' haloed hearts ...

    O Queen of Shepherds!
Carry the purest eau-de-vie
To these workmen while they rest
And take their bath at noonday, in the sea.

The worn-out ideas of old-fashioned poetry played
an important part in my alchemy of the word.

I got used to elementary hallucination: I could very
precisely see a mosque instead of a factory, a drum corps
of angels, horse carts on the highways of the sky, a
drawing room at the bottom of a lake; monsters and
mysteries. A vaudeville's title filled me with awe.

And so I explained my magical sophistries by turning words into visions!

At last, I began to consider my mind's disorder a sacred thing. I lay about idle, consumed by an oppressive fever: I envied the bliss of animals – caterpillars, who portray the innocence of a second childhood; moles, the slumber of virginity!

My mind turned sour. I said farewell to the world in poëms something like ballads:

A SONG FROM THE HIGHEST TOWER

Let it come, let it come,
The season we can love!

I have waited so long
That at length I forget,
And leave unto heaven
My fear and regret;

A sick thirst
Darkens my veins.

Let it come, let it come,
The season we can love!

So the green field
To oblivion falls,
Overgrown, flowering
With incense and weeds.

And the cruel noise
Of dirty flies.

Let it come, let it come,
The season we can love!

I loved the desert, burnt orchards, tired old shops, warm drinks. I dragged myself through stinking alleys, and with my eyes closed I offered myself to the sun, the god of fire.

'General: If on your ruined ramparts one cannon still remains, shell us with clods of dried-up earth. Shatter the mirrors of expensive shops! And the drawing rooms! Make the city swallow its dust! Turn gargoyles to rust. Stuff boudoirs with rubies' fiery powder....'

Oh, the little fly! Drunk at the urinal of a country inn, in love with rotting weeds; a ray of light dissolves him!

I only find within my bones
A taste for eating earth and stones.
When I feed, I feed on air,
Rocks and coals and iron ore.

My hunger, turn. Hunger, feed:
    A field of bran.
Gather as you can the bright
        Poison weed.

Eat the rocks a beggar breaks,
The stones of ancient churches' walls,
Pebbles, children of the flood,
Loaves left lying in the mud.

*

Beneath a bush the wolf will howl,
Spitting bright feathers
From his feast of fowl:
Like him, I devour myself.

Waiting to be gathered
Fruits and grasses spend their hours;
The spider spinning in the hedge
Eats only flowers.

Let me sleep! Let me boil
On the altars of Solomon;
Let me soak the rusty soil
And flow into Kedron.

Finally, O reason, O happiness, I cleared from the sky the blue which is darkness, and I lived as a golden spark of this light, Nature. In my delight, I made my face look as comic and as wild as I could:

> It is recovered.
> What? Eternity.
> In the whirling light
> Of the sun in the sea.
>
> O my eternal soul,
> Hold fast to desire
> In spite of the night
> And the day on fire.
>
> You must set yourself free
> From the striving of Man
> And the applause of the World!
> You must fly as you can ...
>
> No hope, forever;
> No *orietur*.
> Science and patience,
> The torment is sure.

The fire within you,
Soft silken embers,
Is our whole duty –
But no one remembers.

It is recovered.
What? Eternity.
In the whirling light
Of the sun in the sea.

I became a fabulous opera. I saw that everyone in the world was doomed to happiness. Action isn't life; it's merely a way of ruining a kind of strength, a means of destroying nerves. Morality is water on the brain.

It seemed to me that everyone should have had several *other* lives as well. This gentleman doesn't know what he's doing; he's an angel. That family is a litter of puppy dogs. With some men, I often talked out loud with a moment from one of their other lives – that's how I happened to love a pig.

Not a single one of the brilliant arguments of madness – the madness that gets locked up – did I forget; I could go through them all again, I've got the system down by heart.

It affected my health. Terror loomed ahead. I would fall again and again into a heavy sleep, which lasted several days at a time, and when I woke up, my sorrowful dreams continued. I was ripe for fatal harvest, and my weakness led me down dangerous roads to the edge of the world, to the Cimmerian shore, the haven of whirlwinds and darkness.

I had to travel, to dissipate the enchantments that crowded my brain. On the sea, which I loved as if it were to wash away my impurity, I watched the compassionate cross arise. I had been damned by the rainbow. Felicity was my doom, my gnawing remorse, my worm. My life would forever be too large to devote to strength and to beauty.

Felicity! The deadly sweetness of its sting would wake me at cockrow – *ad matutinum*, at the *Christus venit* – in the somberest of cities.

> O seasons, O châteaus!
> Where is the flawless soul?
>
> I learned the magic of
> Felicity. It enchants us all.
>
> To Felicity, sing life and praise
> Whenever Gaul's cock crows.
>
> Now all desire has gone –
> It has made my life its own.

That spell has caught heart and soul
And scattered every trial.

O seasons, O châteaus!

And, oh, the day it disappears
Will be the day I die.

O seasons, O châteaus!

All that is over. Today, I know how to celebrate beauty.

THE IMPOSSIBLE

Ah! My life as a child, the open road in every weather; I was unnaturally abstinent, more detached than the best of beggars, proud to have no country, no friends – what stupidity that was! – and only now I realize it!

I was right to distrust old men who never lost a chance for a caress, parasites on the health and cleanliness of our women – today when women are so much a race apart from us.

I was right in everything I distrusted ... because I am running away!

I am running away!

I'll explain.

Even yesterday, I kept sighing: 'God! There are enough of us damned down here! I've done time enough already in their ranks. I know them all. We always recognize each other; we disgust each other. Charity is unheard of among us. Still, we're polite; our relations with the world are quite correct.' Is that surprising? The world! Businessmen and idiots! – there's no dishonor in being here – but the company of the elect; how would they receive us? For there are surly people, happy people, the false elect, since we must be bold or humble to approach them. These are the real elect. No saintly hypocrites, these!

Since I've got back two cents' worth of reason – how

quickly it goes! – I can see that my troubles come from not realizing soon enough that this is the Western World. These Western swamps! Not that light has paled, form worn out, or movement been misguided. ... All right! Now my mind wants absolutely to take on itself all the cruel developments that mind has undergone since the Orient collapsed. ... My mind demands it!

... And that's the end of my two cents' worth of reason! The mind is in control, it insists that I remain in the West. It will have to be silenced if I expect to end as I always wanted to.

I used to say, to hell with martyrs' palms, all beacons of art, the inventor's pride, the plunderer's frenzy; I expected to return to the Orient and to original, eternal wisdom. But this is evidently a dream of depraved laziness!

And yet I had no intention of trying to escape from modern suffering – I have no high regard for the bastard wisdom of the Koran. But isn't there a very real torment in knowing that since the dawn of that scientific discovery, Christianity, Man has been making a fool of himself, proving what is obvious, puffing with pride as he repeats his proofs ... and living on that alone? This is a subtle, stupid torment – and this is the source of my spiritual ramblings. Nature may well be bored with it all! Prudhomme was born with Christ.

Isn't it because we cultivate the fog? We swallow

fever with our watery vegetables. And drunkenness! And tobacco! And ignorance! And blind faith! Isn't all this a bit far from the thought, the wisdom of the Orient, the original fatherland? Why have a modern world, if such poisons are invented?

Priests and preachers will say: Of course. But you are really referring to Eden. There is nothing for you in the past history of Oriental races. ... True enough. It was Eden I meant! How can this purity of ancient races affect my dream?

Philosophers will say: The world has no ages; humanity moves from place to place, that's all. You are a Western man, but quite free to live in your Orient, as old a one as you want ... and to live in it as you like. Don't be a defeatist. Philosophers, you are part and parcel of your Western world!

Careful, mind. Don't rush madly after salvation. Train yourself! Ah, science never goes fast enough for us!

But I see that my mind is asleep.

– If it stays wide awake from this moment on, we would soon reach the truth, which may even now surround us with its weeping angels! ...

– If it had been wide awake until this moment, I would have never given in to degenerate instincts, long ago! ...

– If it had always been awake, I would be floating in wisdom!...

O Purity! Purity!

In this moment of awakening, I had a vision of purity! Through the mind we go to God!

What a crippling misfortune!

LIGHTNING

Human labor! That explosion lights up my abyss from time to time.

'Nothing is vanity; on toward knowledge!' cries the modern Ecclesiastes, which is *Everyone*. And still the bodies of the wicked and the idle fall upon the hearts of all the rest.... Ah, quick, quick, quick! there, beyond the night ... that future reward, that eternal reward ... will we escape it?

What more can I do? Labor I know, and science is too slow. That praying gallops and that light roars; I'm well aware of it. It's too simple, and the weather's too hot; you can all do without me. I have my duty; but I will be proud, as others have been, to set it aside.

My life is worn out. Well, let's pretend, let's do nothing; oh, pitiful! And we will exist, and amuse ourselves, dreaming of monstrous loves and fantastic worlds, complaining and quarreling with the appearances of the world, acrobat, beggar, artist, bandit – priest! ... on my hospital bed, the odor of incense came so strongly back to me ... guardian of the holy aromatics, confessor, martyr....

There I recognize my filthy childhood education. Then what? ... turn twenty: I'll do my twenty years, if everyone else does.

No! No! Now I rise up against death! Labor seems too easy for pride like mine: To betray me to the world would be too slight a punishment. At the last moment I would attack, to the right, to the left....

Oh! poor dear soul, eternity then might not be lost!

MORNING

Hadn't I *once* a youth that was lovely, heroic, fabulous – something to write down on pages of gold? ... I was too lucky! Through what crime, by what fault did I deserve my present weakness? You who imagine that animals sob with sorrow, that the sick despair, that the dead have bad dreams, try now to relate my fall and my sleep. I can explain myself no better than the beggar with his endless Aves and Pater Nosters. *I no longer know how to talk!*

And yet, today, I think I have finished this account of Hell. And it *was* Hell; the old one, whose gates were opened by the Son of Man.

From the same desert, toward the same dark sky, my tired eyes forever open on the silver star, forever; but the three wise men never stir, the Kings of life, the heart, the soul, the mind. When will we go, over mountains and shores, to hail the birth of new labor, new wisdom, the flight of tyrants and demons, the end of superstition, to be the *first* to adore ... Christmas on earth!

The song of the heavens, the marching of nations! We are slaves; let us not curse life.

FAREWELL

Autumn already! ... But why regret the everlasting sun, if we are sworn to a search for divine brightness – far from those who die as seasons turn. ...

Autumn. Our boat, risen out of hanging fog, turns toward poverty's harbor, the monstrous city, its sky stained with fire and mud. Ah! Those stinking rags, bread soaked with rain, drunkenness, and the thousands of loves who nailed me to the cross! Will there never, ever be an end to that ghoulish queen of a million dead souls and bodies *and who will all be judged!* I can see myself again, my skin corroded by dirt and disease, hair and armpits crawling with worms, and worms still larger crawling in my heart, stretched out among ageless, heartless, unknown figures. ... I could easily have died there. ... What a horrible memory! I detest poverty.

And I dread winter because it's so *cozy!*

– Sometimes in the sky I see endless sandy shores covered with white rejoicing nations. A great golden ship, above me, flutters many-colored pennants in the morning breeze. I was the creator of every feast, every triumph, every drama. I tried to invent new flowers, new planets, new flesh, new languages. I thought I had acquired supernatural powers. Ha! I have to bury my imagination and my memories! What an end to a splendid career as an artist and storyteller!

I! I called myself a magician, an angel, free from all moral constraint. . . . I am sent back to the soil to seek some obligation, to wrap gnarled reality in my arms! A peasant!

Am I deceived? Would Charity be the sister of death, for me?

Well, I shall ask forgiveness for having lived on lies. And that's that.

But not one friendly hand . . . and where can I look for help?

True; the new era is nothing if not harsh.

For I can say that I have gained a victory; the gnashing of teeth, the hissing of hellfire, the stinking sighs subside. All my monstrous memories are fading. My last longings depart – jealousy of beggars, bandits, friends of death, all those that the world passed by – Damned souls, if I were to take vengeance!

One must be absolutely modern.

Never mind hymns of thanksgiving: hold on to a step once taken. A hard night! Dried blood smokes on my face, and nothing lies behind me but that repulsive little tree! The battle for the soul is as brutal as the battles of men; but the sight of justice is the pleasure of God alone.

Yet this is the watch by night. Let us all accept new strength, and real tenderness. And at dawn, armed with glowing patience, we will enter the cities of glory.

Why did I talk about a friendly hand! My great advantage is that I can laugh at old love affairs full of falsehood, and stamp with shame such deceitful couples – I went through women's Hell over there – and I will be able now *to possess the truth within one body and one soul.*

April–August, 1873

A HEART BENEATH A CASSOCK

(The Confessions of a Seminarian)

O Thimothina Labinette! Today, now that I have put on the sacred vestments, I can recall the passion, now dead and cold beneath my cassock, that last year made my heart pound under my seminarian's cloak! ...

May 1, 18 ...

Spring is here. Father ———'s potted vine is sprouting; the tree in the courtyard has tiny buds like green droplets all along its branches; yesterday, on my way out of class, I saw against a second-story window something that looked like the Super's mushroom of a nose. J———'s shoes smell a little; and I notice that the students leave the room quite often to go outside to ———; they used to stay cramming at their studies, buried in books, heads down to their bellies, red faces turned to the stove, breathing hot and steamy breath like cows! Now they stay outside a lot, and when they return, joking unpleasantly, they close the openings in their pants very deliberately – I am wrong; very slowly – and with great ceremony, seeming to take an unconscious delight in an operation which has nothing in it but futility....

May 2 . . .

The Super came down from his office yesterday, and with closed eyes, hands behind him, apprehensive and shivering, shuffled his bedroom slippers for two seconds around the courtyard! Now my heart is beating time within my breast, and my breast beats against my grimy desk! Oh, how I detest the times, now, when we students used to be fat sheep sweating in our dirty clothes, falling asleep in the stinking air of the study hall, in the gaslight and the fitful heat of the stove! I stretch out my arms! I breathe, I stretch out my legs. . . . Oh, I feel things in my head . . . such things!

May 4 . . .

Finally, yesterday, I could stand it no longer! Like the angel Gabriel, I have heard wings in my heart. The breath of the Holy Spirit has transfixed my being! I took up my lyre, and sang:

> O Virgin fair!
> Mary undefiled!
> O Mother mild
> Of our sweet Jesus!
> Sanctus Christus!
> Pregnant Virgin,
> Queen without sin,
> Hear our prayer!

Oh! If you could only know the mysterious exaltations that shook my soul as I plucked the petals of this poetic rose! I took up my kithara, and like the Psalmist I lifted my pure and innocent voice into celestial spheres!!! *O altitudo altitudinum! ...*

May 7 ...

My poetry, alas! has folded its wings, but I say with Galileo, a victim of outrage and torture: And still it moves! (That is, still they move!) I was imprudent enough to drop the preceding inspired lines; J——— picked them up, J———, most savage of Jansenists, most vicious of the Super's henchmen, and he took it in secret to his master; but the monster, to subject me to universal insult, passed my poem around to all his friends!

Yesterday, the Super sent for me; I entered his room and stood before him, calm and strong within. His last red hair trembled on his forehead like a bolt of nervous lightning. His eyes peered from the fat that surrounded them, but calmly and coldly; his enormous nose moved with its usual quiver; he mumbled an *oremus*; he licked the end of his thumb and turned several pages, then took out a dirty, folded piece of paper ...

Maaryyyy Undeeefilllled!
OOOO Motherrrr Miiild!

He was eating my poetry! He was spitting on my rose! He was playing the idiot, the bumpkin, in order to soil, to ravish my virginal song! He stuttered and prolonged each syllable with a cackle of concentrated hate and when he came to the fifth line ... *Pregnant Virgin!* he stopped, contorted his nose, and he ... exploded: *Pregnant Virgin! Pregnant Virgin!* He kept saying it in such a tone, contracting his protruding abdomen with such a shudder, in such an *offensive* tone, that a blush of shame covered my forehead. I fell to my knees, arms stretched to the ceiling, and cried out: 'O father ...!'

'Your lyyyre! Your kithaaara! Young man! Your kithaara! Mysterious exaltations! Shaking your soul! That I would like to have seen! Young man, I find in all of this, in this impious confession, something worldly – a dangerous relaxation of discipline, in fact!' He stopped, and his stomach quivered from top to bottom; then in a solemn tone:

'Young man, do you have the gift of faith?'

'Oh, father, how can you ask such a thing? Are you making fun of me? Yes I believe all the teachings of my mother, the Church!'

'But ... Pregnant virgin! The Immaculate Conception, young man; this touches the Immaculate Conception, the Virgin Birth. ...'

'Father! I believe in conception. ...'

'You do well to do so, young man! It is something....'
He fell silent. Then:

'Young J——— has reported to me that he observes a change in your attitude in study hall; you spread your legs apart, every day more noticeably; he states that he has seen you stretched out at full length beneath the table, in the manner of a young man who ... lacks control. ... These are facts to which you can make no protest. ... Come here – on your knees – close to me; I want to question you quite calmly; answer me: Do you spread your legs often, in the study hall?'

Then he put his hand on my shoulder, around my neck, and his eyes became quite explicit, and he made me tell him things about leg spreading. ... Well, all I can say is that it was disgusting, and I know what scenes like that are all about, too. ...

So they had been spying on me, they had slandered my feelings, misrepresented my modesty – and there was nothing I could say about it, all the reports, the anonymous letters of one student against another, to the Super, since it had all been authorized and directed! And I came to that room, to debase myself at the hands of that dirty old man! Oh, the seminary!

May 10 ...

Oh! My condisciples are terribly wicked and terribly dirty-minded. In the study hall they know everything, the pagans, all about my verses, and the minute I turn my head I see the face of D———, and hear his asthmatic whisper: 'Where's you kithara? Where's your kithara? And your diary?' Then that idiot L——— starts in: 'Where's your lyre? Where's your kithara?' Then three of four of them hiss in chorus:

> Mary Undefiled!
> Mother mild!

What a great dope I am — Jesus, I don't mean to kick myself — but at least I don't tell tales, and I don't write anonymous notes, and I keep my divine poetry and my sense of modesty to myself! ...

May 12 ...

> Can you not imagine why I die of love?
> A flower says to me: hello! ... and a bird above.
> Hello! Spring is here! Angel of tenderness!
> Can you not see why I burn with drunkenness?
> O angel that hung above my baby bed,
> Can you not imagine what runs in my head,
> That my lyre trembles as I beat my wings,
>> And that my heart sings?

I wrote these verses yesterday, during recreation period; I went into the chapel and hid in one of the confessionals, and there my tender poetry was able to revive and fly, in silence and dreams, to the spheres of love. Then, since they are always coming, day and night, to search my pockets for the least little papers, I stitched these verses to the bottom of my inner garment, the one that touches my skin directly, and in the study hall, beneath my clothes, I work my poetry up over my heart, and I hold it tight, and dream. . . .

May 15 . . .

Events have happened so swiftly since last I wrote here, and they are events of such a solemn nature, events which will surely influence my future and my innermost existence in a most awful way!

> Thimothina Labinette, I adore you!
> Thimothina Labinette, I adore you!

I adore you! Let me sing upon my lute, like the divine Psalmist on his psaltery, let me recount how I saw you, and how my heart leapt upon yours to find eternal love!

Thursday was our day off; we can go out for two hours. I went out; in her last letter my mother had written: '. . .go, my son, and spend your free time at the home of Monsieur Césarin Labinette, a close friend of your deceased father, whom you must meet sooner or later before your ordination....'

I introduced myself to Monsieur Labinette, who obliged me greatly by leaving me, without saying a word, in his kitchen; his daughter Thimothina remained alone with me. She took a dish towel and wiped a pot-bellied bowl which she clutched to her heart, and suddenly said to me, after a long silence:

'Well, Leonard?' ...

Until that moment, confused to find myself alone with this young creature in the deserted kitchen, I had kept my eyes lowered and invoked within my heart the sacred name of Mary; I raised my head, blushing, and confronted with the beauty of my questioner, I could only stammer out a feeble: 'Ma'am?'

Thimothina! How beautiful you were! If I were a painter, I would have reproduced your features in canvas and entitled them *The Virgin of the Bowl!* But I am a mere poet, and my tongue can honor you only incompletely ...

The great black stove, with its openings where embers flamed like red eyes, emitted from its delicately smoking cookpots a celestial odor of bean and cabbage soup, and before it, breathing the odor of these vegetables with your sweet nose, with your beautiful gray eyes on your fat cat, O Virgin of the Bowl, you wiped

259

your vase! The smooth light strands of your hair stuck modestly to your forehead yellow as the sun; your eyes continued in a bluish furrow to the middle of your cheeks, just like Santa Teresa! Your nose, full of the smell of beans, raised delicate nostrils; a delicate down winding across your lips contributed not a little to give an energetic beauty to your face; and on your chin gleamed a charming brown spot where madly beautiful hairs quivered. Your hair was soberly pinned on the nape of your neck, but a few short strands escaped. . . . I looked in vain for your breasts; you had none; you were contemptuous of such worldly ornaments! Your heart is your breasts! When you turned around to kick your golden cat I saw your protruding shoulderblades poke your dress, and I was transfixed with love at the sight of the graceful wiggle of the two wide arches of your loins. . . .

From that moment, I adored you. I adored not your hair, not your shoulderblades, not the wiggling of your lower posterior – what I love in a woman, in a virgin, is holy modesty; the thing that makes me leap up with love is modesty and piety; *this* is what I adored in you, young shepherdess!

I kept trying to make her notice my passion, for my heart, my heart was betraying me! I answered her questions only with broken words; several times I called her 'Ma'am' instead of 'Miss,' I was so upset!

Little by little, I felt myself succumb to the magic sound of her voice. Finally I decided to abandon myself, to forgo everything, and so I forget what question she asked me, I leaned back and twisted in my chair, I put one hand upon my heart, with the other I reached into my pocket for a rosary whose white cross I pulled out, and with one eye on Thimothina and the other raised to heaven, I answered sadly and soulfully, like a stag to a doe:

'Yes! Yes! Miss ... Thimothina!!!'

Miserere! Miserere! Into the eye turned so softly to the ceiling there suddenly fell a drop of brine from a pickled ham hung above me, and when, shaken and red with embarrassment and passion, I lowered my head, I realized that in my left hand I held not a rosary but a brown sucking nipple that my mother had given me last year to give to Mrs Whatshername's baby! From the eye that was turned to the ceiling dribbled the bitter brine, but from the one that looked at you trickled a tear, O Thimothina, a tear of love, a tear of bitterness!

Some hour or so later, when Thimothina announced a collation of bacon and eggs and beans, still dazzled by her charms, I answered softly:

'My heart is so full, you understand, that my appetite is ruined!' But I sat down at the table, and oh! I remember it still, her heart answered the appeal of my own; during the short meal, she could not eat:

'Don't you smell something?' she kept repeating; her father didn't understand, but my heart understood; it was the Rose of David, the Rose of Jesus, the Mystical Rose of the scriptures; it was Love!

She got up suddenly, displaying the double flower of her hips, went to a corner of the kitchen, and plunged her arms into a shapeless heap of old boots and shoes and socks, out of which her fat cat jumped, and she dumped all this into an empty closet, then she returned to her place and again investigated the atmosphere with a worried look; suddenly she frowned and exclaimed:

'It still smells!'

'Yes, it does smell,' said her father rather stupidly (he couldn't understand, the animal!).

I was well aware that all of this was but the echo within my virgin flesh of the hidden workings of my passion! I adored her, and I lovingly ate the gilded omelet, and my fork kept time with my heart, and my feet shook with pleasure in my shoes! . . .

But the great flood of light came later, the gage of eternal love, a diamond of tenderness on Thimothina's part – the delightful kindness she showed by offering me as I left a pair of clean white socks, with a smile and these words:

'Do you want these for your feet, Leonard?'

May 16 . . .

Thimothina, I adore thee, thee and thy father, thee and thy cat. . . .

$$
\text{Thimothina} \left\{
\begin{array}{l}
\text{Vas devotionis,} \\
\text{Rosa mystica,} \\
\text{Turris Davidica, } \quad \text{Ora pro nobis!} \\
\text{Coeli porta,} \\
\text{Stella Maris.}
\end{array}
\right.
$$

May 17 . . .

What do I care any longer about the noise of the world, and the sounds of the study hall? What have I to do with those who sit beside me, bowed with laziness and boredom? This morning every head, heavy with sleep, is stuck to the desk before it; like the trumpet call of the last judgment a sound of snoring, a slow and muffled snoring, rises over this vast Gethsemane. I alone, stoical and serene, rise straight above these dead bodies like a palm tree in the midst of ruins. Disdaining incongruous odors and noises, I lean my head into my hand, listening to my heart beat with Thimothina – my eyes plunge into the azure of the sky, through the highest panes of the window! . . .

May 18 . . .

Thanks to the Holy Ghost who has inspired these charming verses; I intend to engrave them in my heart; and when heaven again grants me the sight of Thimothina I shall give them to her in exchange for her socks!

I have entitled this 'The Breeze':

> This cozy cotton bower conceals
> Zephyr wrapped in sweet perfume;
> In a silk and woolen womb,
> Zephyr sleeps with laughing heels.
>
> When the Zephyr lifts his wing
> In his cotton-down retreat,
> When he flies where robins sing,
> His soft breath smells so sweet!
>
> O quintessential breeze!
> O distillate of love!
> Day's dew as it dries
> Perfumes the sky above!
>
> Jesus! Joseph! Jesus! Mary!
> This odor, like a condor's wing,
> Cradles the devotionary . . .
> It sweetens us and makes us sing!

The ending is too personal and too delicate; I shall preserve it in the tabernacle of my soul. On our next day off I shall read this to my divine, my odoriferous Thimothina. Let us wait in calm and contemplation.

Date uncertain . . .
We still wait!

June 16 . . .
Thy will be done, O Lord; I shall put no obstacle before it! If you wish to turn Thimothina's love from thy servant, you are free to do so, of course; but Lord Jesus, have you never been in love? Has the lance of love never taught you to pity the sufferings of the unhappy? Pray for me!

Oh! I waited so long for two o'clock on the fifteenth of June, our day off; I kept my soul in check by telling it that then it would be free! On the fifteenth I combed what modest hair I have, and with a fragrant pink pomade I plastered it across my forehead, like Thimothina's; I put some pomade on my eyebrows, and carefully brushed my black clothes and overcame rather well some embarrassing defects in my appearance, and then went to ring Monsieur Césarin Labinette's long-desired doorbell. He came after a rather long time, his cap stuck over one ear and a strand of stiff pomaded hair stuck to his face like a scar, one hand in the pocket of his yellow-flowered dressing gown, the other on the door latch. . . . He gave me a short good day, wrinkled his nose as he looked down at my black-laced shoes, and went ahead of me, both hands in his pockets pulling his dressing gown in front of him, the way Father —— does with his cassock, so that his posterior is outlined before my eyes. . . .

I followed him.

He went through the kitchen, and I followed him into the sitting room. Oh! That sitting room! It is fastened in my mind with the sharp pins of memory! The carpet had brown flowers; on the mantel was an enormous clock of black wood, with columns, and two blue vases of roses; on the walls, a painting of the battle of Inkerman and a pencil drawing by a friend of Césarin's, of a windmill beside a brook that looked like a trail of spit; the type of drawing that everyone does when he starts to draw. Poetry is decidedly preferable! . . .

In the middle of the room, at a table covered with a green cloth, my heart saw only Thimothina, though next to her was one of Césarin's friends, a former sacristan from the parish of ——, and his wife, Madame de Riflandouille. Monsieur Césarin went to sit down again as soon as I had entered the room. I took an upholstered chair (hoping that some part of me would thus rest on a needlepoint made by Thimothina herself), greeted everyone, set my black hat like a rampart on the table before me, and listened.

I did not say a word, but my heart spoke! The gentlemen continued the card game they had begun. I noticed with a good deal of sorrowful astonishment that each one cheated worse than the other. When the game was ended, we all sat in a circle around the empty fireplace. I was in one of the corners, almost hidden by Césarin's enormous friend, whose chair was all that separated me from Thimothina; I was rather pleased, actually, at the small attention that was paid to me, stuck behind the sacristan's chair, for I could let my true feelings show on my face without anyone seeing them. So I went into transports of joy, and let the conversation go on and on between the other three – for Thimothina spoke only rarely; she flashed her seminarian looks of love, not daring to look him in the face, for she kept her shining eyes on my well-polished shoes! I sat behind the sacristan, and let my passion sweep me away.

I began by leaning toward Thimothina, raising my eyes to heaven. She had turned her back. I shifted a little, and let out a sigh, with my chin on my chest; she didn't move. I fiddled with my buttons, I stuck out my lips; she saw nothing. Then, carried away, mad with love, I leaned far out toward her, holding my hands as at the communion rail, emitting a long and soulful 'ah ...!' *Miserere!* While I was making signs, while I was praying, I fell off my chair with a hollow thump; the fat sacristan turned around with a snicker, and Thimothina said to her father:

'Hey, Leonard just fell off his chair!'

Her father laughed. *Miserere!*

The sacristan put me back up on my stuffed chair, red with shame and weak with love, and then made a place in the circle for me. But I lowered my eyes, I wanted to go to sleep! Their society was unwelcome; they could not imagine the love that suffered there in the shadows. I wanted to go to sleep ... but I realized that the conversation had turned to me....

I opened my eyes feebly....

Césarin and the sacristan were each smoking a thin cigar with the strangest affectations, which made them look awfully ridiculous; the sacristan's wife sat on the edge of her chair with her hollow chest bent forward, spreading out behind her the yellow dress that made her look all puffed out near the neck, and delicately plucked the petals of a rose. A ferocious smile parted her lips and revealed in her gums two teeth, blackened and yellow as the porcelain of an old stove. But you, Thimothina, were beautiful, with your little white collar, your lowered eyes, and your flat hair.

'The young man has a future; the present reflects what will come,' said the sacristan, releasing a cloud of gray smoke.

'Oh, Leonard will be a credit to the cloth,' his wife said through her nose, and displayed her two teeth.

I blushed the way a well-brought-up young man ought to; then I saw them move their chairs apart, and I realized that they were whispering about me. . . .

Thimothina kept looking at my shoes; the two rotten teeth looked threateningly, the sacristan laughed ironically; I kept my head lowered.

'Lamartine is dead,' said Thimothina suddenly.

Thimothina dearest! For your adorer, your poor poet Leonard, you brought Lamartine's name into the conversation; then I raised my head, thinking that only the thought of poetry would reawaken the idea of virginity in these boors; I felt my wings begin to flutter, and I said, beaming at Thimothina:

'Indeed, the author of *Poetic Meditations* bears precious jewels in his crown!'

'The swan of poetry is no more,' said the sacristan.

'Yes, but he has at least sung his swan song,' I continued enthusiastically.

'Ah!' cried the sacristan's wife, 'Leonard is a poet himself! Last year his mother showed me some of the efforts of his muse. . . .'

I acted with boldness:

'Ah, Ma'am, I have neither my lyre nor my kithara with me, but. . . .'

'Oh, your kithara! Well, you can bring it another day. . . .'

'And yet I have this, if it would please the honorable ...' – I pulled a piece of paper from my pocket – 'I would like to read you a few verses ... they are dedicated to Miss Thimothina.'

'Yes, yes, young man. Of course! Recite them, by all means! Do stand there at the other end of the room....'

I stepped back. ... Thimothina kept looking at my shoes ... the sacristan's wife arranged herself like a Madonna; the two men leaned toward one another ... I blushed, cleared my throat, and recited, crooning softly:

> This cozy cotton bower conceals
> Zephyr wrapped in sweet perfume;
> In a silk and woolen womb,
> Zephyr sleeps with laughing heels....

The entire assembly exploded with laughter: the men leaned toward one another and whispered vulgar puns, but the most horrible thing was the look of the sacristan's wife, who sat with her eyes rolled up to heaven, playing the mystic, smiling with her disgusting teeth! And Thimothina ... Thimothina was dying of laughter! I was cut to the core – Thimothina was holding her sides!

'"Zephyr sleeps with laughing heels ...'; that's quite delicate, quite delicate,' said Césarin with a snort.

I began to notice something, then ... but the outburst

of laughter lasted only a moment; everyone became serious again, though they broke down from time to time. . . .

'Continue, young man, continue, that's quite good.'

> When the Zephyr lifts his wing
> In his cotton-down retreat,
> When he flies where robins sing,
> His soft breath smells so sweet! . . .

This time a howl of laughter shook my audience; Thimothina was looking at my shoes; I was terribly hot, my feet burned at her look, I was drowning in sweat; yet I kept saying to myself: The socks I have been wearing for a month are a gift of her love, the looks that cover my feet bear witness to her love; she adores me!

And then a certain indescribable little odor seemed to arise from my shoes. . . . Oh! Then I understood the terrible laughter of the entire group! I realized that fallen into such evil company, Thimothina Labinette, my Thimothina, could never give free rein to her emotion! And I understood, then, that I too would be forced to devour the sad love that had flowered in my heart on a May afternoon in the Labinettes' kitchen, before the wiggling posterior of the Virgin of the Bowl!

Four o'clock, the end of our free day, sounded on the

sitting-room clock; in despair, consumed with love and mad with sorrow, I snatched my hat and fled, overturning a chair, and went along the hallway muttering: I adore Thimothina, but I shall bury myself forever in the seminary ...

The tails of my suit fluttered behind me in the wind, like evil black birds! ...

June 30 ...

From this day on, I leave my sorrow in the hands of my divine muse; a martyr to love at the age of eighteen, I remember in my affliction another martyr to the sex that is our happiness and our joy, and so, no longer possessing the one I have, I shall love religion! May Christ and Mary gather me to their bosom; I shall follow them. I am not worthy to undo the shoelaces of Jesus; but, oh, my agony! Oh, my torment! Even I, at the age of eighteen years, and seven months, bear a cross and a crown of thorns! But in my hand, instead of a reed, I bear a kithara! There lies the balm for my wound!

One year later, August 1 ...

Today, I have put on the sacred vestments; I shall serve God; I shall have a parish and a simple servant in a rich village. I have the gift of faith, I will earn my eternal reward, and without being spendthrift, I shall live like a dutiful servant of the Lord with my house-keeper. Our Holy Mother the Church will comfort me in her bosom: Blessed be the Church! Blessed be God!

... As for that cruelly precious passion that I keep locked in my heart, I will learn how to endure it with constancy: without exactly reviving it, I shall be able sometimes to call it to mind; such things are sweet! (I was born, really, for love and religion!)

Perhaps some day, returned to this same town, I will have the happiness of hearing Thimothina's confession. ... And despite all, I guard a precious memory of her: for a year, I have not taken off the socks she gave me....

O sweet Jesus! I will keep those socks on my feet until I reach the holy gates of Paradise!

RIMBAUD TO PAUL DEMENY
Charleville   May 15, 1871

I've decided to give you an hour's worth of modern
literature. I begin at once with a contemporary psalm:

PARISIAN WAR CRY ... [see page 45]

Here is some prose on the future of poetry:

All ancient poetry culminated in the poetry of the
Greeks. Harmonious life. From Greece to the Romantic
movement – the Middle Ages – there are writers and
versifiers. From Ennius to Theroldus, from Theroldus
to Casimir Delavigne, everything is rhymed prose, a
game, the stupidity and glory of endless idiotic gener-
ations. Racine alone is pure, strong, and great. But had
his rhymes been twisted, his hemistichs messed up, the
Divine Dumbhead would be as unknown today as the
latest-come author of the *Origins*. ... After Racine, the
game gets moldy. It's been going on for two hundred
years!

No joke, and no paradox. My reason inspires me with
more certainty on the subject than a young radical has
fits. Anyway, *newcomers* can swear at their ancestors:
it's their house and they've got all the time in the world.

Romanticism has never been fairly judged. Who's to
judge it? The Critics!! The Romantics? They illustrate
perfectly the fact that the song is very rarely the work
of the singer – that is, his thought, sung and understood.

For *I* is an *other*. If brass wakes as a bugle, it is not its fault at all. That is quite clear to me: I am a spectator at the flowering of my thought: I watch it, I listen to it: I draw a bow across a string: a symphony stirs in the depths, or surges onto the stage.

If those old idiots hadn't discovered only the false meaning of EGO, we wouldn't have to sweep away the millions of skeletons that have for ages and ages piled up the products of their one-eyed intelligence, and acclaimed themselves their authors!

In Greece, as I said, words and music gave a rhythm to Action. Afterward music and rhymes became toys, pastimes. Studying this past has a certain charm for the curious: some people delight in reworking these antiquities: that's their business. The universal intelligence has always cast off its ideas naturally; men would pick up some of these fruits of the mind: they were acted upon, they inspired books: and so it went; man didn't develop himself, not yet awake, or not yet aware of the great dream. Pen pushers, these writers: the author, the creator, the poet; that man has never existed!

The first task of the man who wants to be a poet is to study his own awareness of himself, in its entirety; he seeks out his soul, he inspects it, he tests it, he learns it. As soon as he knows it, he must cultivate it! That seems simple: every brain experiences a certain natural development; hundreds of *egoists* call themselves authors; there are many more who attribute their intellectual progress to themselves! – But the problem is to make the soul into a monster, like the comprachicos,* you know? Think of a man grafting warts onto his face and growing them there.

I say you have to be a visionary, make yourself a visionary.

A Poet makes himself a visionary through a long, boundless, and systematized *disorganization* of *all the senses*. All forms of love, of suffering, of madness; he searches himself, he exhausts within himself all poisons, and preserves their quintessences. Unspeakable torment, where he will need the greatest faith, a superhuman strength, where he becomes among all men the great invalid, the great criminal, the great accursed – and the Supreme Scientist! For he attains the *unknown!* Because he has cultivated his soul, already rich, more than anyone! He attains the unknown, and if, demented, he finally loses the understanding of his visions, he will at least have seen them! So what if he is destroyed in his ecstatic flight through things unheard of, unnameable: other horrible workers will come; they will begin at the horizons where the first one has fallen!
    – Back in six minutes –

*The 'comprachicos' (in Victor Hugo's *L'Homme qui rit*, published in 1869) were kidnappers of children. They deformed them into freaks in order to exhibit them. (tr. note)

I interrupt my discourse with another psalm: be kind enough to lend a willing ear, and everybody will be delighted. Bow in hand, I begin:

MY LITTLE LOVELIES ... [see page 66]

There. And please note that if I were not afraid of making you spend more than 60 centimes on postage due – poor starving me who hasn't had a single centime in the last seven months! – I would send you also my 'Amant de Paris,' one hundred hexameters, and my 'Mort de Paris,' two hundred hexameters.

Here we go again:

The poet, therefore, is truly the thief of fire.

He is responsible for humanity, for *animals* even; he will have to make sure his visions can be smelled, fondled, listened to; if what he brings back from *beyond* has form, he gives it form; if it has none, he gives it none. A language must be found; besides, all speech being idea, a time of universal language will come! Only an academic – deader than a fossil – could compile a dictionary, in no matter what language. Weaklings who begin to *think* about the first letter of the alphabet would quickly go mad!

This language will be of the soul, for the soul, and will include everything: perfumes, sounds, colors, thought grappling with thought. The poet would make

277

precise the quantity of the unknown arising in his time in the universal soul: he would provide more than the formula of his thought, the record *of his path to Progress!* Enormity becoming norm, absorbed into everything, he would truly become a *multiplier of progress!*

That future will be materialistic, as you see. Always full of *Number* and *Harmony*, these poems will be made to last. Essentially, it will again be Greek Poetry, in a way.

This eternal art will be functional, since poets are citizens. Poetry will no longer give rhythm to action; it *will be in advance.*

And there will be poets like this! When the eternal slavery of Women is destroyed, when she lives for herself and through herself, when man – up till now abominable – will have set her free, she will be a poet as well! Woman will discover the unknown! Will her world of ideas differ from ours? She will discover strange things, unfathomable, repulsive, delightful; we will accept and understand them.

While we wait, let us ask the *poet* for *something new* – ideas and forms. All the bright boys will soon think they've answered us: but that's not it!

The first Romantics were *visionaries* without completely realizing it: the cultivation of their souls began accidentally: abandoned locomotives, still running down the tracks – Lamartine is sometimes a visionary, but strangled by old forms. Hugo, *too thick-headed*, has had many visions in his latest volumes: *Les Misérables* is a real poem. I have *Les Châtiments* at hand; *Stella* gives some measure of Hugo's *vision*. Too much Belmontet and Lamennais, too many Jehovahs and columns, old worn-out enormities.

Musset is fourteen times abominable for this present generation of pain, obsessed by visions – whom his angelic laziness has insulted! Oh, those insipid *contes* and *proverbes*! His *Nuits*! His *Rolla*, *Namouna*, and *La Coupe*! It's all so French, that is, hateful to the highest degree; French, not Parisian! Another work of that same genius that inspired Rabelais, Voltaire, Jean de la Fontaine, commentaries by M. Taine!

Vernal, Musset's mind! Charming, his love! Here it is, painted on enamel, real solid poetry! French poetry will be enjoyed for a long time – but only in France. Any grocery boy can reel off a *Rolla*, every seminarian has five hundred rhymes in a secret notebook. At the age of fifteen these flights of passion give young boys hard-ons; at sixteen they recite them with *feeling*; at eighteen, at seventeen even, every schoolboy who can write a *Rolla* writes a *Rolla*! It probably still kills some of them. Musset couldn't do anything worthwhile; there were visions behind those lace window curtains; he closed his eyes. French, stuffed, dragged from café to schoolroom, the beautiful corpse is a corpse – and from now on let's not even try to wake it up by yelling at it!

The second generation of Romantics are real visionaries: Théophile Gautier, Leconte de Lisle, Théodore de Banville. But to examine the invisible and hear the unheard is something else again from reviving the spirit of dead things, so Baudelaire is the first visionary, the king of poets, *a real God*. And still he lived in too artistic a milieu; and his highly praised form is silly. The inventions of the unknown demand new forms.

Stuck with the old forms: among the idiots, A. Renaud – wrote his *Rolla*; L. Grandet – wrote his *Rolla*; the Gauls and the Mussets: G. Lefenestre, Coran, Cl. Popelin, Soulary, L. Salles; the schoolboys: Marc, Aicard, Theuriet; the dead and the imbeciles: Autran, Barbier, L. Pichat, Lemoyne, the Deschamps, and the Des Essarts; the journalists: L. Cladel, Robert Luzarches, X. de Ricard; the fantasists: C. Mendès; the bohemians; the women; the talents, Léon Dierx and Sully-Prudhomme, Coppée. The new school, called Parnassian, has two visionaries, Albert Mérat and Paul Verlaine, a real poet. There.

So I am working at making myself a visionary. And let us close with a pious hymn:

SQUATTING ... [see page 61]

You'd be a bastard not to answer; quick, for in a week I'll be in Paris – maybe.

Goodbye,

A. Rimbaud

INDEX OF FIRST LINES